"Because I experienced so much good in intensive weeks and conversational groups with Blessing Ranch Ministries, I knew this book would be helpful. But the fresh lens and step-by-step journey offered here by Drs. Byers and Walker FAR exceeded my expectations. They have done in writing what I thought might only be done in person. Anyone who is done settling for less than God's dream for them will be masterfully helped to discover unexpected freedom, connect deeply with others, and create fresh space and intimacy with God as He writes a better story in their lives. I am, once again, forever grateful for their help found here."

—Drew Moore, Lead Pastor, Canyon Ridge Christian Church

"*You don't NEED counseling; you DESERVE counseling.*' When I heard this phrase, it immediately resonated and shaped my view of having wise voices speak into my life. Dr. Walker and Dr. Byers have not only spoken into my life but have put together in this book what God has done in and through them for over 25 years at The Blessing Ranch. If you need someone to speak life into your soul, deal with your hurt and find a new way forward. Then this won't be just a book you 'need' but a book that you 'deserve.'"

—Nate Ross, Lead Pastor, Northside
Christian Church, New Albany, IN

"Laura and I are deeply indebted to the wonderful ministry of Drs. John Walker and Charity Byers. Over the years, we have sent both staff and dear friends who have greatly benefited from their warmth and wisdom. When we walked through our darkest hour, the loss of our 17-year-old son, they were the first voices that God used to begin our healing journey. We are truly grateful that they have put their lives' work into this inspirational book. We are supremely confident that *Unhindered* will transform countless lives as it has our own."

—Robert and Laura Koke, Lead Pastors
Shoreline Church, Austin, TX

"Wouldn't it be great if our lives could be lived without conflict or heartache? Sadly, none of us get that life! So what do you do when the story of your heart is interrupted? You begin the process of transformation, and healing. I have found that process much more meaningful and beneficial with a little help. I have personally benefited from the wisdom of Dr. Charity Byers and her father Dr. John Walker. I have spent hours with them gleaning from their knowledge, and working toward a deeper spiritual maturity. The principles they use in their counseling program have been provided in this book, and I know that, regardless of where you are on your journey, the tools presented here will help you and those you love."

—Holly Wagner, Founding Pastor, Oasis Church, Founder, She Rises, author of *Find Your Brave*, and a girl on her journey with God!

"Unhindered is a must read! Many of us who love Jesus feel deep down in our hearts, that something is hindering us from living the life we know we should be living. Often, there's a huge gap between who we want to become and who we currently are. This book is a gift from God to help us close that gap. The principles that John and Charity have written have helped me overcome years of battle weariness,

leadership pain, and betrayal. This book is a breath of fresh air, even a lifeline for those who want to be totally free and live lives that are completely *Unhindered*.

—Kenneth J. Claytor, Senior Pastor, Alive Church
Gainesville & Orlando, FL, author of *One Race: How A
Church That Resembles Heaven Can Heal Our Racial Divide*

"Over the years, as a leadership consultant, I've had the honor of serving amazing leaders. Often though, they would be at inflection points in their personal lives foreseeably taking them down an undesirable pathway. In almost all those situations I have recommended the ministry of Blessing Ranch. One hundred percent of the people I have referred to Blessing Ranch have been helped, and they've found personal wholeness. This book *Unhindered* by John Walker and Charity Byers will help us all align the stories of our hearts."

—Sam Chand, Leadership Consultant and
author of *Leadership Pain* (*samchand.com*)

"When you employ the hearts of counselors and add the mind of a theologian and multiply it by the experience of a multi-generational ministry of 25 years, you get a book like *Unhindered*. For all those who help others and for those in need of help, *Unhindered* is a must have. Get it and be blessed. Read it and live!"

—Michael Pitts, Founder/Bishop, Cornerstone Church

"We've been big fans of Dr. John and Dr. Charity for some time. They've counseled, coached, and helped restore countless marriages (including our own) with their prolific wisdom and biblical insights on relationships. You gotta love their humble and calming approach—plus their distinct ability to slap you upside of your head with the truth you need to hear. 'WOW! Okay...this is really gonna change our lives!' If peace and trust are things you crave in your relationships, then we encourage you to follow the roadmap in *Unhindered* and discover 'the story of your heart.'"

—David Crank, Author, Senior Pastor, *FaithChurch.com*,
Nicole Crank, Author, TV Host, Senior Pastor, *FaithChurch.com*

"I'm not just an endorsement for this book; I'm the poster child. It's not an overstatement to say that I might not still be in ministry or married if it weren't for Blessings Ranch Ministries. So when they asked me to read a preview of the book that unlocks the code, I jumped at the chance. John and Charity help us bridge the gap between who we are and the best version of us—the one God intended—by allowing God to edit our stories. They don't let us off the hook (They never let me off the hook!) because it's not some magic formula; it's a joint effort. But I\we need guidance for our side of the equation. I know this book is written by two very smart people, but I promise you this: If they can help me, they can help anyone! I highly recommend this book to you."

—Tim Harlow, Senior Pastor, Parkview Christian
Church, Author of *Life on Mission: God's People Finding God's
Heart for the World* and *What Made Jesus Mad? Rediscover
the Blunt, Sarcastic, Passionate Savior of the Bible*

"John and Charity have given us the keys to overcoming our brokenness and living in the fullness of whom God has made us. Based on a lifetime of helping Christian Leaders through their darkest times, *Unhindered* provides a comprehensive Biblical approach to enjoying freedom from our brokenness and living out God's perfect plan for our lives. This book is essential for every Church Leader, not only as a personal resource but also as a Spirit-breathed manual on how to help the multitudes that come broken and looking for wholeness. *Read* this book before you ***need*** this book."

—Ben Woods, Programming Executive, Hillsong Channel

"*Unhindered* is a brilliant book that can reshape your story and refocus your purpose. Charity Byers and John Walker have helped thousands of people, including me, learn how to reframe our lives in healthy ways that honor God and others. Here they pull the curtain back and reveal their learnings about how we can allow God to rewrite our storie with faith and confidence. This will be one of the most important books you ever read!"

—Jud Wilhite, senior pastor, Central Church, author, *Pursued*

Cover design by: Joe DeLeon

ISBN: 978-1-950718-74-0   1 2 3 4 5 6 7 8 9 10

Printed in the United States of America

Unhindered

*Aligning the Story
of Your Heart*

—

CHARITY BYERS, Ph.D.
JOHN WALKER, Ph.D.

AVAIL

CONTENTS

Opportunity for a Deeper Dive

As you read this book, you'll be challenged to look inward and think about your heart and your life in ways you may not have before. We know it can be a daunting challenge, and we want to give you resources to do it well.

We are publishing an assessment instrument that will serve as a valuable counterpart to this book. It will help the content of this book come alive in a personal way. It will help you identify the specific pieces of your heart that are hindered and need to be submitted to God's healing and growth processes. We hope you'll get excited about this opportunity to learn about your story and catalyze your learning and growth.

This assessment instrument reports on the wide range of topics covered in Chapters 2 through 9 of this book. The in-depth instrument asks you to respond to over 200 items that report on 6 major scales and 58 subscales. Once psychometrically validated, this instrument will be available in the spring of 2021. You can look for details at *www.TrueWiring.com/Unhindered*.

Introduction

"I've always handled things pretty well, but in the last few months, I feel like I'm carrying a 10-ton weight."

"I snap. I snap at my husband. I snap at my kids. I snap at my friends and at people at the office. This isn't me, but I can't stop myself."

"I know I should be over my divorce so I can move on, but I'm not. It's weighing on me every day. My kids see it. I'm afraid I'm ruining their lives."

"I don't know what to do. My life seems to be spinning out of control. I've tried everything, but nothing works."

"What my dad did to me happened so long ago. Shouldn't I be over it by now?"

"I've lived a secret life. I can't tell anybody about it. If they knew, they'd never trust me again."

"Things are pretty good overall, but I really want to go from good to great in my leadership."

"I trust God, but I sense Him asking me to trust Him even more and I don't know how to jump that hurdle."

"I'm exhausted, and I think I'm going to burn out. If I don't find the freedom to do some things differently, I don't know how long I can keep going."

"My spouse and I are roommates at this point. I've wondered if I married the wrong person. I used to think we could be so much more, but when we're not fighting, I feel alone and empty."

A s we've talked with thousands of people over the years, we've heard the full range of stories: hope and disappointment, joy and grief, peace and anxiety, supportive relationships and shattered ones. Some come to us because their lives are spinning out of control, and they desperately need someone to help them find solid ground. Others come because they're doing well, and they want to be better spouses, parents, and leaders. They trust us to give them the principles and skills they need.

Whatever your background and whatever your current situation, the concepts in this book apply to you. Over the past several decades, we've studied many fields of human behavior, and God has given us what we believe to be significant insights into the way He has made us. He has led us to craft solutions we believe are sound, both psychologically and spiritually. And we assure you: You're not our guinea pig! We've used these concepts with thousands of people. Without their affirmation that God has used the principles to change their lives, we certainly wouldn't be writing this book.

The metaphor you'll find throughout these pages is "story." All of us have a story, one we call "the story of your heart." Our stories have been written by past relationships, shaped by important events, and deeply ingrained in our hearts and minds. For some of us, the stories have been written by parents who loved us and gave us "roots and wings"—roots of security and wings to try new things without the fear of failing. But others have very different stories, written in heartache and edited by fear and doubt.

God is willing—no, He longs—to edit your story, to replace fear with faith, doubt with confidence, and resentment with love. The astounding truth is that God will heal your deepest wounds and turn them into your greatest strengths. They become the source of your genius. As the Spirit of God, the Word of God, and one or two skilled people of God help us identify the hurts we've tried to avoid our whole lives, we can experience more love, kindness, forgiveness, and strength than we ever imagined. Then, we'll have a deep well of compassion to notice others' hurts and step into their lives. We can give them what God has given us—peace, hope, joy, and love.

Most authors would shudder at the idea of having their raw, unedited work put on display for the world to read. That's why authors submit their original work to an editing process—the current version is simply not as good as it could be. It's just a rough draft, an unrefined and unpolished version. Perhaps the original draft lacks clarity or relevance. An author wisely submits his or her writing to an editing process to correct mistakes, clarify the message, and make it more powerful. Authors trust that an editor will make their work better—but they need to give their manuscripts to the right editor.

When God edits our stories, He carefully crafts them to be more like His original intention for us. He has always had a wonderful story for each of us, but our flaws and the flaws of others have made it hard to read.

Here's what God intended: The story of your heart began with the pen in the hands of God. He was the writer who lovingly and carefully crafted a flawless story for your heart. He was the original creative, the one who gave birth to the vision for you.

When God created you, He made you in His image (Genesis 1:27). That means the story He originally wrote reflects His glory, majesty, and beauty. He put the best elements He could imagine into it, such as trust, hope, peace, belonging, esteem, humility, and security. It is a story woven with the threads of God's perfect truths and purposes. When He was done, He pronounced it "very good" (Genesis 1:31), and it made Him smile.

The story God wrote for your heart speaks of His unique design for you and reflects the fullness of His goodness. His story leads you to a more abundant life (John 10:10), brimming with impact (Ephesians 2:10). In this story you have no artificial, internal barriers to hold you back. You aren't tethered by self-doubt, a compulsion to control, performing to prove yourself, image-management, anger, bad habits, or anything else that stands in your way. You live freely, love lavishly, and leave the world better than you found it. We call this "wholehearted living."

If we could go back to the Garden and experience God's original story for us, we would experience the wonder of unfettered love, peace, joy, and strength. We wouldn't just read about them; we'd inhabit them. Sounds good, doesn't it?

But there's a problem . . . a big problem. God is committed to our free will, and gave the writing process to us. To say the least, we've written bad manuscripts! Sin, ours and others, has distorted the message, caused immeasurable harm, and left us fearful and confused, driven to be on top, compulsive to please people to earn their approval, or shrinking in fear from any perceived threat. Still, no matter how poorly our stories have been edited by us and others around us, God promises that He will edit them to be much closer to His original intention.

What was and is God's intention? Former seminary president Cornelius Plantinga writes that the effect of sin "isn't the way things are supposed to be." He summarizes God's purpose for us in the concept of *shalom*:

> The webbing together of God, humans, and all creation in justice, fulfillment, and delight is what the Hebrew prophets call shalom. In English we call it peace, but it means far more than just peace of mind or ceasefire between enemies. In the Bible, shalom means universal flourishing, wholeness, and delight—a rich state of affairs in which natural needs are satisfied and natural gifts fruitfully employed, a state of affairs that inspires joyful wonder as its Creator and Savior opens doors and speaks welcome to the creatures in whom he

> delights. Shalom, in other words, is the way things are
> supposed to be.[1]

Is the shalom story of your heart still possible? You can't go back
to the Garden, but you can invite God to edit your existing story so
that it more closely resembles His original intentions. When the current story of your heart is edited by God, He writes beauty, peace,
strength, and joy into it.

But . . . will we ever get back to the original story? Yes, absolutely!
Scripture tells us that the arc of God's story for mankind is this: creation, fall, redemption, and restoration. The story in Genesis began
in a perfect garden, and the story ends in Revelation in a perfect city:
the new heavens and new earth. There, all sin, sorrow, and death will
be obliterated. Tears will be turned to shouts of joy. We'll experience
unfettered delight in the presence of God, and we'll celebrate with
each other. God will give us roles that are full of meaning. That's what
God intended for Adam and Eve, and it's His promise to us.

But for now, we live between "the already" and the "not yet."
Some of the promises of God—the ones of forgiveness, identity, and
the Holy Spirit's presence—have already been granted to those who
believe. But other promises—the complete restoration of creation,
freedom from the presence of sin, and a face-to-face relationship with
God—won't come in this life. We have to wait for them, but we wait
with a confident hope.

Does it really matter that the current story of your heart needs
God's edits? Yes, undoubtedly! The story of your heart determines
the trajectory of your life. You, as the main character, live what has

---

1   "Sin: Not the Way It's Supposed to Be," Cornelius Plantinga, Jr., The Henry Center, https://
henrycenter.tiu.edu/wp-content/uploads/2014/01/Cornelius-Plantinga_Sin.pdf

been written on your heart. God's editing process may rewrite certain chapters and could even alter the ending. No one can write a better story than God. The story that has already been written, and the one you're continuing to write, are missing some of the goodness, wisdom, love, and strength God yearns to write into it. But something within you is standing in your way. Fear? Pride? Self-pity? Shame?

God is waiting with pen in hand to edit your story so that you can reach the unhindered life waiting for you. Living a life unhindered means being able to rise to the next level of emotional and spiritual health so that you can get beyond the barriers you've never been able to cross. It means finding the capacity to live and love a little more like Jesus by experiencing His love, forgiveness, and acceptance so much that these beautiful qualities overflow into the lives of others. It means being able "to live freely and lightly," even in the midst of this difficult world (Matthew 11:28-30, MSG).

Yes, it's possible to hand the pen to God and watch Him rewrite our stories. The process can be daunting, so we want to give some important advice: Don't do this alone. In our experience, it's easy for people to become confused, to feel frustrated, and to give up too soon. Find someone who has been down this path before: a counselor, a sponsor, a support group, or a friend who has experience in this level of insight and growth. As you take steps, realize that the Holy Spirit is your advocate and guide. Trust Him to reveal things that have been hidden in darkness—not to condemn you but to invite you into a process of hope and healing.

We've written this book to show you how to hand the pen to God. In these pages, we'll give you a strategic pathway to redeem the story of your heart and discover the unhindered, free, beautiful life waiting for you. Don't settle for a hindered life full of fear and confusion; join us in partnering with God as He rewrites our stories.

CHAPTER 1

The Story of Your Heart

Our ideas form the belief system upon which we base our actions and decisions, and these in turn determine the trajectory of our lives. Living a life without lack involves recognizing the idea systems that govern the present age and its respective cultures— as well as those that constitute a life away from God—and replacing them with the idea system that was embodied and taught by Jesus Christ.

—DALLAS WILLARD

I (John) grew up in a family that was loving and good, but hard work with no excuses and no complaining, along with a Christian commitment, was the essence of our family life. When I was very young, an injury led to repeated times of humiliation, especially in school, and planted seeds of fear and inadequacy deep inside me. It taught me to be afraid of being seen as stupid, and consequently, to always over prepare. I had no idea this was my secret coping strategy, and neither did anyone else. Everyone who saw me assumed that I was just a good kid who seemed to have it all together.

In my adult life, this process morphed into a need to be seen as thoroughly competent and to achieve success in everything I attempted. Validation from others was always significant; nevertheless, it was always short-lived. I was only as good as my last performance. This led to a lot of pressure and anxiety. It also led to me becoming increasingly private because I didn't want anyone to see that my outward portrayal and my inward experience didn't match. But some others saw me as a "perfect phony"—arrogant and prideful.

Nothing showed this more clearly to me than the honest, yet hard-to-swallow feedback my classmates gave me when I was in my master's degree program. They said, "John, you're just unlikeable. You present yourself as so perfect and put together. We know that no one is that perfect, so we just can't believe it."

The story that God had for me was completely different from the "perfect phony" story. He had a story for me built on security in my heart and security in my life. I had to learn that God had gifted me with wisdom and ability far beyond my capacity. I discovered the truth that my achievement wasn't for me but for others. It was my service. My willingness to pay a high price wasn't so that I could receive validation; it was so that I could go the extra mile to come alongside to help people. The healing that took place showed me that I have nothing to fear and nothing to be ashamed of. Consequently, there's no need to hide. I can use my voice, stick my neck out and take great risks for the kingdom of heaven. I'm courageous and strong, God is with me, and I can trust Him even when I don't understand and can't control or fix problems. My true genius in Christ is my willingness to "show up" and know that it's more than enough.

Some people may still not like me, and I may not get it right every time, but at least I'm not a phony.

From the beginning of your life, you've been primed for meaning and love. Unconsciously, you've been furiously taking notes as you've experienced life. You've been trying to discover who you are, who God is, who people are, and what the world is all about. You've internalized spoken and unspoken messages. In fact, you've been a sponge soaking up everyone's mood, words, and actions, especially in the formative years of your childhood.

As you've interpreted meaning through interactions and circumstances, words were written on your heart. Before long, you began to draw conclusions and define meaning. As accumulated experiences affirmed this meaning, the words grew into themes, sentences, and chapters. The writing continued until one day a dominant story emerged, a story that carries your deepest meanings. It's the story of your heart.

Your story is much more than a tale of feelings. It's the narrative of your identity—who you believe you are.

It's more than an account of your life experiences. It's the story of how your experiences have shaped you.

It is more than a picture of the visible life you lead. It gets behind the scenes to explain what's buried deep inside you, driving you and guiding you.

The story of your heart is guiding you—in fact, far more than you know. You may think you're a bunch of randomly collected feelings, habits, inclinations, and proclivities, but you're far more cohesive than that. The story of your heart bonds together what's within you and what flows out of you. Proverbs 4:23 says, "Above all else, guard your heart, for everything you do flows from it." Proverbs 27:19 echoes that saying, "As water reflects the face, so one's life reflects the heart." The story of your heart is the "meta-narrative," the big story of who you are: how you relate to people, your drives and passions, the ways you defend yourself and hide from hard truths, and why you respond the way you do.

Few of us take the time to uncover our story, but it must be understood. Only when we see it clearly and understand its power will we have enough perception to allow it to be rewritten. Getting beyond where we are now won't come from trying harder, being more disciplined, or changing our circumstances. It will come by handing the pen to God and joining Him as He edits our story.

The Edits

Two versions of your story—your current one and God's edited story—are competing for ownership of your heart. As we've seen, your current story has been written by the influences of an imperfect world that has departed from God's original purpose and plan. The writing performed by flawed people—ourselves and others—has moved the trajectory of your life away from the goodness God envisioned for you. Your current story leaves you vulnerable to convincing whispers of the enemy that you're unloved, unlovable, and incompetent. These messages make you settle for less than God's best. They tell you to give yourself a pass on one or two of the fruits of the Spirit, perhaps thinking that your faithfulness should be enough to cover up your lack of kindness or courage. Your story disguises fear as safety and pessimism as realism. With this distorted story, you may know the truth of God, but it doesn't create a beautiful blend of humility and passion. Instead, it's a life that leads to exhaustion, defeat, and friction. You're content to survive instead of thrive. It may be a life of utter destruction if you use extreme ways to deaden the pain and control people, it may drive you to achieve to prove yourself, it may compel you to compensate for your insecurity by dominating others, or it may be an emptiness of withdrawing from any threat of conflict or failure, and settling for a bland life.

God's edits include, to some degree, the beauty and goodness He originally planned for you. You're able to see yourself through His eyes, not your own. You push against artificial limits that have held you back from the impact God intends you to have. The fruits of the Spirit (Galatians 5:22-23) flow from you without strenuous effort or faking them. You easily find your way to trust and hope, which leave you resilient when life tries to beat you up. It's not a perfect life, but it's a life that flows from God's truth planted deeply in your heart, not just in your head.

On the next two pages are two illustrations of the story of your heart. One is the story that has been written by flawed authors, compromising your ability to live freely and lightly and forcing you to try all kinds of strategies to block the pain and gain power or acceptance. The second is God's edited story—full of truth and goodness. You'll see that the story of your heart is made up of several elements, such as Heart Shapers, Sore Spots, and Life Outcomes. Each of these elements comes together to create a story. Many of the terms are probably unfamiliar to you, but as the chapters of the book unfold, you'll examine each of the elements that make up the story of your heart and discover the redemptive process that takes place as God edits your story.

The Hindered Heart

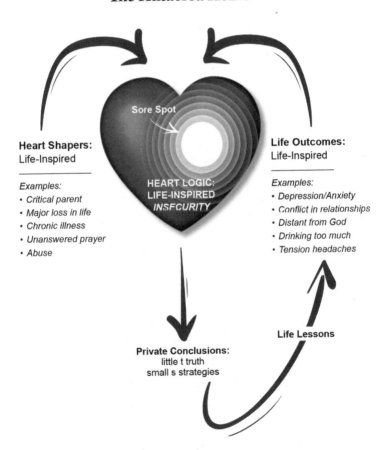

Sore Spot

Heart Shapers:
Life-Inspired

Examples:
• *Critical parent*
• *Major loss in life*
• *Chronic illness*
• *Unanswered prayer*
• *Abuse*

HEART LOGIC:
LIFE-INSPIRED
INSECURITY

Life Outcomes:
Life-Inspired

Examples:
• *Depression/Anxiety*
• *Conflict in relationships*
• *Distant from God*
• *Drinking too much*
• *Tension headaches*

Life Lessons

Private Conclusions:
little t truth
small s strategies

The Unhindered Heart

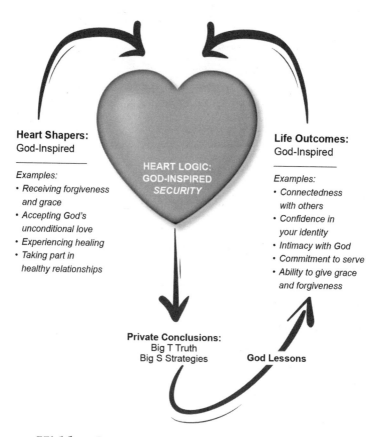

Heart Shapers:
God-Inspired

Examples:
- *Receiving forgiveness and grace*
- *Accepting God's unconditional love*
- *Experiencing healing*
- *Taking part in healthy relationships*

HEART LOGIC:
GOD-INSPIRED
SECURITY

Life Outcomes:
God-Inspired

Examples:
- *Connectedness with others*
- *Confidence in your identity*
- *Intimacy with God*
- *Commitment to serve*
- *Ability to give grace and forgiveness*

Private Conclusions:
Big T Truth
Big S Strategies

God Lessons

Hidden Barriers

For too many of us, our stories are dramas—but not in a good way. We try hard, and we make strides toward Christ, but along the way, we hit points where we stall out. Maybe we've trusted in Christ, but there's a piece of us that has a nagging doubt about His love, or we can't bring ourselves to cooperate with what we know God is asking of us. It's not a lack of desire. Something else, something previously hidden from us, is standing in the way.

We live in an imperfect world that has more influence on our hearts than we'd like, even when we wholeheartedly love Jesus.

We're a decidedly mixed bag, full of competing impulses. We want to follow God, and we want to run from Him; we love Him, but we love comfort, pleasure, prestige, power, and possessions, too. God's image in us is tarnished, but it's still there—even if we have a hard time uncovering it.

God knew very well that His intended story would be compromised in a tragically flawed world. It's part of the human condition. But the story isn't finished. With your cooperation, God can edit the story of your heart, so it reads more like His original vision.

The Story of My Heart

God meant for me (Charity) to be a leader, but I didn't know it for the first 30 years of my life.

I was a shy kid. On the first day of kindergarten, I asked my mom if I could sit in the back by myself. The scariest thing was to be seen and noticed. I liked the shadows.

Even though I came out of my shell to some extent as I grew up, I still tried to keep part of me hidden. I developed great friends, got good grades, and made every sports team I tried out for. Nevertheless, I was afraid for people to really see me. I can remember despising questions like, "What's your favorite movie?" I'd immediately think, "I don't know. What *should* my favorite movie be?" In high school, I was utterly embarrassed when my friends gave me a hard time for a car accident that was my fault. Mistakes like that flooded me with shame. I wanted to push them out of my mind as fast as possible. Later, when I figured out that alcohol could help me avoid the insecurity, shame, and pain, I started using it often as a tactic to feel numb. I was too ashamed to ask for help and failed miserably trying to fix it on my own.

For many years, the echoes of insecurity haunted me.

Nevertheless, there was a boldness within me. When I got on the starting block to swim a race, I wasn't going to let anyone tell me I couldn't win. But when it came to revealing my heart, I was sure I was going to lose.

The boldness of that little ten-year-old on the starting blocks was a glimmer of my true self, the story God wanted to write for me. Even though shyness was a natural part of who I was, God never intended for me to be dominated by shame. He never wanted me to doubt myself. He never meant for me to hide and hold back.

God had to edit the story of my heart so that I could learn what it means to walk boldly in the Spirit and how to let the voice of the Spirit flow through me.

I sometimes still hear those voices of self-doubt. My first instinct is to hide, but God has revealed His vision for me, and I won't turn back. Every day I choose to declare, "I am bold!" It seems that Joshua 1:9 was written for me: "This is my command—be strong and courageous! Do not be afraid or discouraged. For the Lord your God is with you wherever you go" (NLT).

Do You Know the Story of Your Heart?

We're sure you know a lot of stories, but do you know the story of your heart?

Knowing the story of your heart isn't a matter of simply tracking all the events of your life to see a timeline emerge. Your heart contains a deeper story, a dramatic story of hope fulfilled and hope denied, of love enjoyed and love crushed, of strong faith at times and no faith at others.

Some don't know how to tell their story. All they can see are the problems, strained relationships, and broken dreams. With a little insight, they realize their unhealthy, even self-destructive, responses to people and situations make perfect sense when they understand their flawed story.

Some don't want to acknowledge the narrative of their story because it's too painful, so they bury it and pretend it's not there.

And others think it's pointless to examine their hearts. They don't think they've been impacted by the accumulation of experiences from their past.

Your experiences have written a story in your heart, and the story must be told. Only when you understand your story will you trust God and hand Him the pen. Your unhindered life awaits—it's the place without the heavy burdens like performance anxiety, self-loathing, unholy discontent, and an unhealthy need to control.

More Than Sin

As you begin to uncover your heart's story, you may instantly focus on sin as the root of all evil in your life. Sin certainly is evil, but it's not always the root of your dysfunction. There can be far more than sin that's influencing your story.

The writer of Hebrews gives us layers of insight: "Therefore, since we are surrounded by such a great cloud of witnesses, let us throw off everything that hinders *and* the sin that so easily entangles. And let us run with perseverance the race marked out for us" (Hebrews 12:1, emphasis added). Before he identifies sin as a problem, he warns us to avoid "everything that hinders" us. This is a broad category that includes good but secondary things like approval, comfort, prestige, and power, and it also includes pain, shame, fear, and resentment that have twisted the story of our hearts.

Here are some "things that hinder" us:

- Fear
- Self-doubt
- Mistrust
- Anger
- Selfishness
- Self-reliance
- Rejection
- Arrogance
- Shame
- Inadequacy
- A thirst for power
- A compulsion to control
- Being a people-pleaser

Some of these may lead you down a path of sin, or they may limit your capacity for leadership, love, or faith. Ridding our lives of sin isn't enough. While that's necessary, we must go beyond that and eliminate the hindrances that keep us from experiencing all that God has for us.

The Gaps

Jesus gave us many wonderful promises, including this: "I came so they can have real and eternal life, more and better life than they ever dreamed of" (John 10:10, MSG).

As psychologists, we hear stories from people in all walks of life. Some are in the middle of a crisis. Others want to take the next step in their development or fine-tune one aspect of their lives. We hear stories from leaders, caregivers, pastors, CEOs, volunteers, and teachers, among many other roles. Some are new to faith, and others have been walking with God for decades. While the people and their positions in life are all unique, they share one thing. They all have gaps. You have one, too.

A gap is a chasm between *who you are now* and *the best version of you*—the one equipped to live out of your full capacity for the glory of God. A gap is the distance between the current you and the beauty beyond description God envisioned when He created you.

Your gap is between your current story and God's unhindered story for your life. Each time flawed influences write another word, sentence, paragraph, or chapter, the gap becomes wider and keeps you farther away from wholehearted living.

The gap shows up in tangible ways that are both external and internal: emotionally, relationally, spiritually, behaviorally, and physically.

The gap in your life might look like this:

Emotional Gap:
- You can't get past the critical voice in your head.
- You feel overwhelmed by expectations, sure you'll never measure up.
- You dream of feeling joy but spend most days discouraged and disappointed.
- You know the truth that God loves you, but you still don't feel lovable most of the time.
- You can't extend that grace to yourself that you freely give to everyone else.

Relational Gap:
- You're tired of feeling alone, but you can't let people in.
- You don't want to be so irritable and angry with the people you love most.
- You keep putting up with mistreatment in a relationship.
- You desperately try to earn approval by saying the right thing and doing the right thing, but you always beat yourself up for being such a loser.
- You struggle to be vulnerable because you're convinced the person, or even vulnerability, isn't safe.

Spiritual Gap:
- You can't let God have control because you don't trust that He has your best interests in mind.

- You're having trouble trusting God, and that's created a barrier between Him and you.
- You're consumed with all you have to do to connect with God.
- You know God says He's loving, but you keep seeing Him through the lens of your earthly parents and may not even realize it.

Behavioral Gap:
- You know you're capable of the next level of leadership, but you just can't get there.
- You want out of the addiction, but it has you in its grip.
- You continually second-guess yourself, and therefore, hold back too much.
- You feel paralyzed by performance anxiety.
- You have to be in control by dominating or enabling; you may be afraid of feeling out of control, or you may want people to need you as validation that you're significant.

Physical Gap:
- Worry is keeping you from sleeping at night and getting needed rest.
- The constant, unrelieved pressure is causing headaches, stomach problems, bruxism, and other stress-related problems.
- You have problems with your weight, and you don't exercise.
- You don't value yourself enough to invest in self-care.

- You're exhausted because you won't slow down or take breaks.

Character Gap:

- You say family is priority, but you continually put your success above yours.
- You lack integrity by carefully hiding your struggle with lust or greed.
- You get defensive far too easily and can't take ownership of your mistakes.
- Your pride causes you to take credit that's due to others and soak up the spotlight that should be shared.
- You claim it's love, but it's really manipulation.

After noticing your gap, you might look around and say, "How is this my life?" Or you may say, "I'm doing okay, but there's probably more for me." Many of us secretly long for more—more peace, more joy, more security, more belonging, more impact. Whether or not you've known it, you have a gap.

Your Relationship with Your Gap

As you identify your gap, you have to decide how you're going to address it. Over the years, we've helped people close their gaps. In doing so, we've noticed four common responses to gaps. Which one best describes you?

1. You fall into the gap.

Those who have fallen into the gap are utterly frustrated with it but throw their hands up in defeat. They live with the nagging realization that they're missing out on the best in life. They're frustrated, but they have no idea what to do about it.

2. You befriend the gap.

Those who have befriended the gap have accepted their lives as "good enough." Instead of making their gap their enemy and conquering it, they've made it their friend. It gives them a convenient excuse to avoid making hard decisions or trying something new. Some have gone numb, and others have lowered their standards and hidden behind the defiant excuse, "That's just who I am. Get over it."

3. You deny the gap.

Those who deny the gap have intentionally put blinders on, often because it feels too uncomfortable to acknowledge it. Honesty requires courage, and these people simply don't have enough courage to face the facts. They claim they don't have a gap, that life is good, and there's no need to change. Some are misguided by the pop trend to "be yourself" and see it as a license for whatever comes naturally.

4. You're ready to mind the gap.

If you've ridden the railway in the United Kingdom, you've probably seen the signs: "Mind the Gap." You hear the phrase in a distinctly British voice at every stop, and you see it painted on the station platforms in front of the doors. The phrase is calling passengers to take

action—to manage the dangerous gap between the train door and the
station platform.

Those who want to mind their gaps recognize the danger
and are ready to overcome it, even if at first they don't know how.
They're willing to give the pen to God and partner with Him to edit
their stories.

All of us need to mind our gaps because we're all capable of being
more than we are right now.

Static or Changing?

In *Soultsunami*, theologian and pastor Leonard Sweet writes,
"What is the difference between a living thing and a dead thing? In
the medical world, a clinical definition of death is a body that does not
change. Change is life. Stagnation is death. If you don't change, you
die. It's that simple. It's that scary."[1]

For some, the gap feels like a canyon. For others, it feels more like
a crevice. But sadly, many don't even see their gap. Their life's motto
is, "It is what it is. Don't worry about it." But their gap is real.

Being a healthy person isn't a static condition. Healthy people
change, and in fact, healthy people get healthier. Being a Christian isn't
a static condition either. In his letter to the Philippians, Paul assured
them, "And I am certain that God, who began a good work within you,
will continue his work until it is finished on the day when Christ Jesus
returns" (Philippians 1:6, NLT). God is always calling us to a more

---

1   Leonard Sweet, *Soultsunami* (Grand Rapids: Zondervan, 2009).

authentic character, greater maturity, and more effectiveness. With God, there is always bigger, better, and greater.

Even those who are in the process of overcoming the tragedy of abuse or abandonment are called to more. Maybe you've come to Christ and left an unhealthy lifestyle behind, or maybe it still haunts you. Maybe you've already dealt with a nagging trust issue or low self-confidence, and you feel healthier than you've ever been, or maybe you're just more skilled at hiding your self-doubt.

Perhaps you trust God when things are going well, but you don't trust Him (or anyone else) when you encounter any significant risk. Or maybe you've stopped exploding at others but still have a gnawing bitterness inside of you. For all of us, there's always another layer of healing, development, or refinement.

If you feel like you're emotionally and spiritually healthy and life is good, you might wonder if we're trying to uncover problems when there aren't any. This isn't an appeal to become dissatisfied with your life! Actually, an unhindered life can be derived from a place of contentment that's married with passion for the next step. However, in our experience, virtually every person we've met has an ungrieved loss, an unhealed wound, or an unforgiven offense that's left him or her with a hang-up.

The purpose of this book is to give you hope that change is possible and provide skills to help you take steps forward. Letting God edit your story requires enormous courage, but we assure you, it's worth the effort.

Some people misinterpret God's promises. Instead of joy and hope, they feel anxiety and guilt. If it seems that His call to be more and do more is an indication that God will never be satisfied with you, please understand this: God delights in you just where you are (Zephaniah 3:17). No matter how big the gap is in you, hear God's simple invitation to take the next step.

Rickety Bridges

You need a way across your gap into a better life and a better you. Without being equipped with the right processes to mind the gap, we try to use all kinds of rickety bridges to get across.

You may think that the way to a better life is to simply change your circumstances or to change other people. That's a rickety bridge. When you have problems, you point fingers at your circumstances and at other people's behavior, and shout, "If he would just stop doing that, I could stop doing this!" or "If she weren't in my way, I'd be happy."

As pastor and author John Ortberg quotes Dallas Willard: "If your soul is healthy, no external circumstance can destroy your life. If your soul is unhealthy, no external circumstance can redeem your life."[2] Changing external circumstances is a rickety bridge that won't get you across your gap.

Another rickety bridge is to lean on disciplines without understanding the motives underneath them. You might do your best to become more like Christ by reading your Bible, praying, fasting, serving, or giving. Those practices are certainly good for your soul, but they're not magic. If you do them to earn points with God or

---

2 John Ortberg, *Soul Keeping* (Grand Rapids: Zondervan, 2014), p. 40.

to impress people, they can do more harm than good. Can you tell the difference?

We also run into problems when we don't use the disciplines to specifically address the core issues. People may be learning all kinds of spiritual truths, but if they haven't uncovered their true motives and deep wounds, they can't allow spiritual truths to deeply challenge the core issues and become the source of change they are meant to be. You need to be specific and targeted in practicing the disciplines, so they let God right into your wounded place.

Having God edit the story of your heart is the only solid bridge across the gap. Full authorship of your heart's story must be returned to God, so it can become a beautiful, unhindered story.

Jesus reminds us that God's story is the one that will bring us the rest, relief, freedom, and joy we've been looking for: "Are you tired? Worn out? Burned out on religion? Come to me. Get away with me and you'll recover your life . . . . I won't lay anything heavy or ill-fitting on you. Keep company with me and you'll learn how to live freely and lightly" (Matthew 11:28-30, MSG).

The Partnership

More times than I (John) can count, I've talked with Christian leaders who have told me, "Yes, I have this problem with anxiety (or anger or selfishness or comparison or any of a dozen other nagging issues). I've prayed and prayed that God would take it from me, but He hasn't. In fact, it's only gotten worse. I've asked Him to heal me, to deliver me, or do whatever it takes to free me, but I'm still haunted by it."

I don't tell them they're crazy. Who wouldn't want to be freed from the shame of a heart that seems impervious to the work of the Spirit? But with a heart of kindness born from personal experience, I tell them, "If you don't mind, I'd like to tell you something I've learned. I believe that's the wrong prayer." At that moment, they often look at me like I've told them I'm a Martian, but I continue. "I don't believe God wants to immediately free you, or He would have already answered your prayer. Instead, I believe He wants to walk with you and teach you lessons you wouldn't learn from complete and instantaneous relief. God wants to partner with you in the deep transformation of your heart. It won't be quick, but it will be better than you've ever imagined."

This is one of the most important themes of this book. We're trusting God to edit our stories, and we hand the pen to Him, but we have to hold the paper. We're in it with Him, and He's in it with us.

As I look at the Scriptures, I see this pattern again and again. Here are a few instances:

- Luke tells us about 10 lepers who asked Jesus to heal them. He told them, "Go, show yourselves to the priests." On their journey, they were cleansed. Only one returned to thank Jesus, but all 10 were healed when they took steps of obedience (Luke 17:11-19).
- John describes a scene when Jesus and the disciples passed by a man who had been blind since birth. The disciples (like most of us) immediately wanted to find the cause and pin

the blame. They asked, "Rabbi, who sinned, this man or his parents, that he was born blind?" Jesus explained that God had bigger plans than they knew. He made some mud from dirt and spit, and told the man to wash in the Pool of Siloam. He did, and he received his sight. The man had to take action for the miracle to happen (John 9:1-6).

- Mark takes us to a synagogue where Jesus saw a man with a withered hand. He told the man, "Stand up in front of everyone." Jesus used this moment to rebuke the Pharisees who were too hardhearted to care for the man on a Sabbath. Jesus told the man, "Stretch out your hand." As he stretched it out, his hand was healed. The man could have said, "I'm not going to stand up or stretch out my hand. You can heal me without me doing anything," and he would have been right, but Jesus involved the man in his own healing (Mark 3:1-6).

- In a striking Old Testament story, Naaman, the general of the king of Aram, an enemy of Israel, had a terrible skin disease, probably leprosy. A captured slave girl told him that Elisha could heal him, so he traveled to Israel. His first stop was to see Israel's ruler, who was so distressed with the request that he tore his robes. He sent Naaman to Elisha, who sent his servant to tell the general, "Go to the River Jordan and immerse yourself seven times. Your skin will be healed and you'll be as good as new" (2 Kings 5:10, MSG). Naaman was furious that Elisha didn't come out and instantly heal him, and he was angry that he had been instructed to wash in the Jordan instead of the great rivers of his homeland. But finally, after some encouragement from his attendants, Naaman dunked himself seven times in the Jordan, and he was healed. Sometimes, we don't like the instructions we're given to be God's partners. We think we have a better way, but when we obey, God works.

- After Paul writes (or quotes) a beautiful hymn about the humility and glory of Christ in his letter to the Philippians, he gives them this insight about trust: "Therefore, my dear friends, as you have always obeyed—not only in my presence, but now much more in my absence—continue to work out your salvation with fear and trembling, for it is God who works in you to will and to act in order to fulfill his good purpose" (Philippians 2:12-13). We don't work for our salvation, but we work out our salvation—with awe that God would partner with us, with obedience to do what He instructs, and with hope that the power of the Spirit will accomplish God's good purposes.

The pattern we see in these (and many other) passages is straightforward: trust, obedience, deeper trust, and glad submission to the will and ways of God. In an incredible mark of God's grace, He invites you and me to join with Him in the process of change—in our lives and in the lives of others.

I'm passionate about this principle because it has been instrumental in my life. From the time I was a boy in middle school, I felt called to preach, but an event that happened a few years earlier changed my heart's story. Late in the summer when I was seven years old, I stepped on a board, and a rusty nail went through my shoe and into my foot. Usually, this kind of injury isn't a big deal, but my foot got infected, and I developed what then was called "blood poisoning," now known as sepsis. I almost died. Gradually, I recovered, but I missed the first weeks of school. I'll tell more of the story later in the book, but for now, let me just say that I was behind my classmates in every subject, and some of them made fun of my mistakes. At that point, the hole in my sole became a hole in my soul, and I vowed that I'd be sure my performance never opened a door for anyone to make fun of me again.

As I grew up and became a pastor, the fear of others' disapproval consumed me. I saw every Sunday as a courtroom; the congregation was the jury, and I had no idea what the verdict might be. I was afraid—no, I was terrified—that I'd prove once and for all that I wasn't good enough. My defense was to prepare, and I mean to the nth degree. I hoped that being completely ready, having carefully thought through every point and practiced them all, would give me the security and confidence I lacked. It didn't. My fallback was to ask God to deliver me from my performance anxiety. He didn't. My fear was amplified as I watched preachers who could fly into a city on Saturday afternoon with a few notes scribbled on a napkin from the plane, and deliver some of the richest, most beautiful and powerful sermons I've ever heard. It was painfully obvious that I wasn't one of them.

My typical MO was to sit as hymns were sung and announcements made before I went to the pulpit. During that time, I went over and over my message, changing points, adding new ideas, subtracting lines that suddenly seemed irrelevant, and rehearsing the first six lines so I could guarantee a good start. Every week, my not-quite-articulated but very real prayer was, "Oh God, please don't let me screw up today!" My chief goal was to keep from being embarrassed—or at least, not too embarrassed. I hoped God would just zap me and free me from my rampant performance anxiety, but He never did.

One Sunday as I went through my rigid and grueling routine, I uttered a different prayer: "Oh, God, may I join with you today to accomplish your purposes." That may not sound like a cataclysmic change, but it was. In fact, it was one of the most important turning points of my life. I sensed God was saying, "Yes, John, I'll be your partner. Trust me more than your preparation."

Throughout this book, you have choices. You can hope God will step in and zap you to complete healing, confidence, and joy, but in my experience, that's incredibly rare. Far, far more often, He invites us to be His partner in the process. It's our sincere privilege, and it's our great responsibility.

God's Story in a Difficult World

Of course, even when we invite God to edit our stories, we still live in a broken world with broken people. Difficulties come knocking at the door. Do you even make it through one day without feeling challenged, a little beat-up, or discouraged in some way? Probably not.

Life's circumstances challenge us. Some of them are dramatic, such as when a tragedy takes down the most precious person you know, or the most-feared diagnosis turns out to be true. But many of them are everyday annoyances, like the feelings of failure when something didn't turn out like you'd hoped, a child's demands get the best of you, or when it feels like your prayers are bouncing off the ceiling.

When life is too much for us, we usually just want it to settle down. But what if it doesn't? What if the real solution isn't for life to settle down but for us to rise up? Maybe life doesn't need to be easier. Maybe we need to be wiser and stronger.

This kind of strength can only come from the new story God edits.

God's version of your story gives you anchors when life tries to rip your security from you. It gives you a better name to call yourself than the one others have given you. It gives you a source of hope when life has turned dark. It leaves you with a sense of belonging when you feel abandoned. It helps you take on life's challenges as opportunities rather than as handicaps. It may even make your circumstances begin to look a little brighter, even if they don't change.

Difficulties are unavoidable, so how will you respond? Will you take major hits, accumulate deep wounds, and get derailed? Or will you rise up because God has written a better story deep in your heart? Will you be able to pick yourself back up, see beyond your difficult circumstances, and demonstrate resilience when life presses in?

God's edited story of your life is your best weapon against "everything that hinders and the sin that so easily entangles" you (Hebrews 12:1).

Hand Over the Pen

Can you hear God's voice calling? What's He calling you to be and do? Is He asking you to be honest about your deepest wounds or darkest secrets so He can bring His healing touch? Is He calling you beyond timid faith to bold faith? Do you have the sense that He's challenging you to greater leadership? Is He calling you to love more selflessly or give more generously?

Can you remember the dreams you once had about the way your life would turn out? The way *you* would turn out? The impact you would make on the world? Maybe you haven't thought about them in a long time because you've settled for what's average, normal, and bland. Or maybe those dreams haunt you every night and have become a constant reminder of your failure. Your dreams might be almost tangible to you, but you might just have no idea how to mind the gap. Maybe you've even forgotten how to dream.

What you see in yourself today is a glimmer of what God sees in you. When your heart is more fully living out His rewritten story, it will release goodness and godliness that you didn't know existed. You'll preserve all of the good that's already in you, and you won't be enslaved to artificial limits, pain, or self-sabotaging behavior. You'll fire on all cylinders and reach even more deeply into your God-gift-edness so that you can unleash your impact on the world.

So, hand over the pen to God, so He can rewrite the imperfect pieces of your heart's story.

The Pathway to God's Edited Story

As you continue reading, you're going to discover the process that hands the pen to God. The pathway doesn't depend on changing your life; it depends on changing your heart. If you follow the pathway, you won't have to aimlessly wander any longer toward a better life.

The promise may sound too good to be true. Some of you already want to put this book back on the shelf because it sounds a little too much like a "health and wealth" promise. But when it sounds too good to be true, sometimes it's God. What if God wants to get your attention to show you His process for creating an unhindered life in you?

We don't intend to offer you shallow hope for a better life. We want to ask you the questions you didn't even know to ask, so you can be healed in ways you didn't know you needed to heal. We want to get to the true heart of the matter—the edits God wants to make to your story. This is the pathway to genuine and lasting transformation that comes from the inside out. This is the pathway to wholehearted living.

You may think you'll never get there, but you can. God wrote the same original story full of security, trust, esteem, and belonging for you that He wrote for us and for everyone else in the world. You might feel a long way from that original story, but God hasn't abandoned you. He'll pick up the pen if you'll give it to Him.

Your job is to submit your heart to His editing process, a process of healing and transformation that conquers the pain of the past and trusts in God's words and ways. Allow God's healing touch into the deepest places of your heart so that His truths can have their rightful power.

Find the courage to look inward, experience change from the inside out, and watch God write a better story for you.

At the end of each chapter, you'll find some questions to help you reflect more deeply about the concepts. Don't hurry through these.

There's not a prize for finishing first! Take time to think and pray, and consider using these questions in conversations with your spouse, a friend, a small group, or someone else you trust.

Reflection

Why did you pick up this book? What do you hope to get out of it?

Describe how the story of your heart has been written up to this point in your life. Who had the pen? What did he or she write? What's your current story?

Review the list of the gaps. What's the gap in your life?

How are you dealing with your gap? Have you fallen into it? Are you befriending it? Are you denying it?

Picture your unhindered life. What are three things waiting for you there?

Have you ever gotten the order backwards and tried to rewrite the story of your life in order to rewrite the story of your heart? How did that work?

Does it encourage you or discourage you that God is inviting you into a partnership for your transformation? Explain your answer.

CHAPTER 2

Heart Shapers

While God is in the heart-shaping business, so much more than God has shaped your heart.

—REGGIE MCNEAL

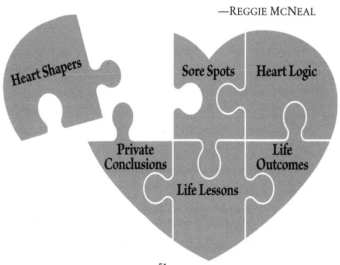

A s Jane was rewriting her heart's story during her time at Blessing Ranch Ministries, she wrote this during one of her reflection times:

Take a deep breath and remember who You Are!!!

My home wasn't loving. My environment was critical and filled with bickering. It became my world, and I numbed out to deal with the anxiety. I couldn't feel because it would've been too overwhelming. Nevertheless, I was always afraid of being in trouble, because in one form or another, trouble was all around me even though it wasn't often directed towards me. When I believe I'm in trouble and that it's really directed at me—I panic, and that brings out the worst in me.

This fear of always being in trouble has followed me throughout my adult life, more than I've realized, and it became my normal. It's caused me to be a people pleaser and a fixer, always believing it would somehow make people like me...accept me...appreciate me. The only problem is that it used to work to prevent trouble, but it actually creates trouble now. It hasn't worked for a very long time. It's been hard to realize that, but it's true! Avoiding conflict creates conflict. Fixing often leads to more harm than I've known. Blind affection causes me to truly be blind, left only with pretending. This has led me to be a "good girl" in the worst sense of the words—"BEING TAMED." This is not me! This is not who I was created to be!!!

So who am I really? I'm a Warrior Princess who uses her voice to make her home, her family, and this world better. I'm full-on crazy in that pursuit—I tell the truth unapologetically, I have a good heart, and I know my worth, I'm soft and strong, full of genuine compassion and affection, I practice ruthless trust. I am ruled by God's love, not fear. I live the gospel day-to-day. I was born to be wild, and I'm dangerous. I'm the type of woman you want to go to war with, not against. I'm not perfect, but I'm HOLY. I was created to make a real difference. I WILL REMEMBER THIS ALWAYS!! THIS TRUTH SETS ME FREE, FREE INDEED!!!

At the start of her time at Blessing Ranch, Jane could hardly acknowledge that her family of origin wasn't all good. Any criticism of it felt like blaming and exaggerating because she believed she was loved, even loved deeply. It took much prodding and prompting for her to be honest about the way she felt in that critical environment and understand what it did to her heart. When she could finally see the power that was held by her old eggshell environment, she could connect the dots between her early experiences and the grip of desperately trying to please people to win affection. For the first time, she could believe the "tamed good girl" wasn't all she was capable of being.

Her insight into her early life was the crucial beginning of her awakening.

Insight is essential. You can't rewrite a story that hasn't yet been told.

Even though it's yours, the story that you're about to tell may not sound very familiar. It goes far beyond the surface of your life and looks deep inside. So, put aside what you think you know about yourself and give God an opportunity to reveal what He wants you to know.

The story of your heart consists of six elements that are woven together: Heart Shapers, Sore Spots, Heart Logic, Private Conclusions, Life Lessons, and Life Outcomes. The next several chapters will help you understand each element and show you the pathway to rewriting your story.

In Chapter 1 we said that you aren't just a random accumulation of thoughts, feelings, and actions. The different parts of you are more cohesive than you might think, and all of them are important parts of your heart's story. Your emotions, moods, beliefs, and behaviors are like branches whose health is dependent on the health of the roots (i.e. your heart) that give them life. (If this weren't true, you'd have many more problems of mental illness to manage!)

For example, you might look at your life and see a constellation of problems that don't seem to have much in common: (1) you have terrible boundaries with others and let them walk all over you, (2) you feel overwhelmed by working too hard, and (3) you beat yourself up all the time. If you see these problems as unrelated, you're likely to feel confused and give up before you even start trying to solve them! But all of these are integrally connected beneath the surface, and the connection is insecurity.

When insecurity tells you that you aren't enough, you may let others have inordinate power over you so you don't risk losing their acceptance, or you may react in the opposite way, trying to intimidate and dominate people to control them. You might overextend yourself to prove your value through your performance, or you might be too hard on yourself, convinced you're just a screw-up. Each of those problems stems from the deepest parts of your heart's story where insecurity has been written.

Connecting the dots back to the roots in your heart can bring remarkable relief! You can finally understand why you react the way you do, and even more importantly, you can identify the singular pathway forward: healing the insecurity in your heart. But connecting the dots requires courage—the brutal truth is the only place where lasting change can be found.

Relief will only come when you turn your insecurity into security—a security in who you are by God's description, not your own. This seemingly small but monumental change will alter the trajectory of your life. With the new root of security, you'll be able to use your voice and advocate for yourself, and you'll quiet the critical voice inside you. That's a huge difference powered by the change of one word in your heart's story.

Prepare for a journey of understanding that will help you connect the dots and see your strategic pathway forward.

The first step is to understand how your heart has been shaped. This is the first element in the story. You have to see beyond what has happened to you and learn to read the narrative of how what happened affected you.

Heart Shapers

What's written on your heart isn't an accident. The words and sentences have been shaped by people and events, both painful and pleasant.

We can learn a lot from Scripture about the heart. The word *heart* is used 570 times in the NIV Bible, and it is most often used metaphorically to describe the inner self, just as we're defining it, the place where feelings, thinking, longings, and willpower meet. The biblical writers often refer to the heart as the place of our personhood, our true selves. Through Scripture's descriptions, we gain insight into the multidimensional influences that mold the story our hearts. We call these "Heart Shapers."

Heart Shapers are the forces that propel the pen into motion. The heart takes in all of the information from these influences and stores it, synthesizes it, and ultimately makes meaning from it. And when something has enough force behind it, the pen moves, writing a message on your heart.

Heart Shapers inevitably make marks on your heart. They either write more clearly the powerful and beautiful story God has for you, or they distort the truth of God's love, forgiveness, power, and joy, leaving you insecure, frantic, and defensive.

It all depends on who holds the pen.

With the help of Scripture, we have identified ten categories of negative forces that shape our hearts. In the table below, we give some examples of each category. For the purposes of this book, we aren't giving attention to the positive influences, though we fully acknowledge they exist. But it's the negative influences getting in your way that need light to be shined on them.

You'll also notice that the ten categories are organized into two sections: Primary Heart Shapers and Secondary Heart Shapers. Primary Heart Shapers are straightforward. They are tangible and easily identified. They also tend to be the most powerful in shaping our hearts. Secondary Heart Shapers often affect us covertly. They can be described as moderating variables. They're not events or experiences but foundations within us that impact the state of our hearts.

As you examine these categories of Heart Shapers, we hope that you can acknowledge that who you are today is not all an inevitable product of your DNA. Your environment had a big impact on you.

Primary Heart Shapers:

1) *Everyday life experiences*: Moments that may not stand out individually but accumulate into messages that matter.
   Negative examples: A relationship ending, losing a job, disengaged spouse, repeated criticism, unattainable expectations

2) *Family*: The lessons, patterns, and impacts derived from a family of origin.
   Negative examples: Sibling rivalry, absent parent, explosive anger in the home, harsh or inconsistent family rules, abuse, abandonment, critical environment

3) *Defining Moments*: Individual events that have extremely strong impact for good or for bad. These can include "God moments" and mountaintop experiences as well as traumatic events.

Negative examples: Abuse, divorce, infidelity, death, major illness, significant loss

4) *Biology*: Your nature, personality, physical characteristics, DNA.
Negative examples: A disability that impacts your experience and identity, a predisposition to depression or anxiety, a driven nature

5) *Sin/Evil*: Your sin, others' sin, spiritual warfare.
Negative examples: Giving in to temptations, moral failures, sinful thoughts, impacts on us from the sins of others

Secondary Heart Shapers:

1) *The Mind*: The way you think, understand, process, and perceive the world around you.
Negative examples: Black and white (all or nothing) thinking, rigid thinking, biased thinking

2) *Beliefs*: Your spiritual convictions, guiding principles, moral compass, and anchor points.
Negative examples: Unbiblical theology, immoral standards

3) *The Emerging Self-Concept*: What you learn about who you are, how you see yourself, an emerging self-concept.

Negative examples: Deciding "I'm stupid" after a failure, concluding "No one wants me" after a rejection, judging "I'm defective" after a continued struggle

4) *Emotions*: Feelings and passions, the affective side of us, how our feelings attach meaning to life.
Negative examples: Being dominated by emotions, the influence of stuffed or unexamined emotions, the overwhelming state of emotions that leads to meaning making

5) *The Will*: Volition, desires, motivation for choices, the cognitive side of us that attaches meaning to circumstances and relationships.
Negative examples: Insatiable will toward something—"I'll get whatever outcome I desire no matter the cost." "I'm always confused, but I must have an answer and a plan." "I know better than anyone—including God—how my life ought to go, and I'll make it happen."

Your Heart Shapers have written the existing story in your heart. All of us have a blend of drama, tragedy, love, and maybe some comedy, too. But, for many, the stories have far too much drama and tragedy.

The Imperfect Teacher

Experience can be a great teacher. If you're trying to learn how to hit a baseball, there's no substitute for stepping up to the plate and feeling the way the bat connects with the ball. Or if you want your children to learn to behave, sometimes you have to let them experience the consequences of bad choices.

Experience can be an excellent teacher in matters of skill, but it's often an unreliable teacher in the matters of the heart. For some of us, our life experiences have taught our hearts something that reflects the loving character of God. But far too often, painful experiences teach us that we're unloved, unsafe, and incompetent—and these lessons sound like absolute truth.

Pain Steals the Pen

As you've gone through life, you've had hundreds of Heart Shapers writing the story of your heart, and they've picked up the pen every day. Your heart is always watching and listening, even when you aren't aware of it. You might say we have a "sixth sense" about Heart Shapers.

Among all that input, you encounter plenty of confusing or contradictory messages your heart has to navigate. You might have competing input between a parent who says you're very talented and a teacher who says you don't have anything to offer—or the other way around. God says it's safe to trust Him, but your experience tells you never to let your guard down. Perhaps you got fired from a job for lacking skill, but another company snatched you right up, affirming your competence.

What will have the power to press the pen into motion, and what will we reject?

It's not usually a matter of what you *want* to absorb and what you don't, but rather what has *intrinsic power* over your heart. And unfortunately, painful experiences have immense power to reshape your story. Actually, many of us screen the input, but we let negative messages in and reject the positive ones. We practice "confirmation bias" and accept only the messages that reinforce what we already believe. For instance, if we already believe we're unworthy and unwanted, those are the only messages we hear (or think we hear) from every source— even God.

Pain can reshape your heart's story in an instant. Sometimes a single shattering event ruins the beautiful story God intended for you. But pain also writes a dark drama through a series of hard knocks or corrosive statements that build up and form a powerfully destructive message.

Dismissing the Power

In our conversations with our clients, we've noticed that many people check out when we start talking about pain. Some roll their eyes and feel like we're wasting their time when we ask questions about their family of origin and their most important life experiences. They think they haven't had any significant pain, or they've concluded that what happened to them was too long ago to be a big deal now. We're certainly glad they haven't been completely overwhelmed by a hard life, but they still need to realize they've experienced pain. All of us have, but not many of us have learned to process it in a positive, healthy way.

Our distorted thoughts about pain can be so ingrained that they've become myths we consider to be completely true and valid. The myths are designed to perform one function and achieve one goal: to prevent us from having to open the Pandora's box of hurts from the past and be honest about them. Do you believe any of these myths that need to be challenged?

Myth #1: *Difficult or painful things that happened in the past don't affect me now.*

Some live with the fallacy that their hearts are impenetrable and difficult things don't bother them. They'll say things like, "That happened so long ago that I hardly remember it." Or they minimize and say, "It was hard, but many people had it far worse." We appreciate their attempts to avoid being a wimp who can't handle anything hard, but all of us have to acknowledge that pain, suffering, and imperfection are part of life outside of Eden. No one gets an exemption card.

Author Richard Rohr notes, "Pain that is not transformed is transferred." Pain exerts influence on your heart long after the dust has settled. After the crisis is over and the intensity of the pain has subsided, the effects of pain linger. The saying that "time heals all" simply isn't true. Time may take the edge off, but what pain has written on your heart exerts its subversive influence until it is surfaced, addressed, grieved, and healed.

Being affected by past pain doesn't necessarily mean that you're in such agony that you don't want to get out of bed in the morning because you're depressed or that you can't turn the tears off—though plenty of people are affected in those ways. You don't have to be in deep agony to be deeply shaped. Someone who has made peace with a divorce that happened in her family 30 years ago can still have her guard up, unwilling to let anyone in for fear of being left and crushed again.

Many people need their eyes opened to the sneaky ways unnoticed pain is influencing their lives. We all have to accept that being affected by pain doesn't make us weak; it makes us human.

Myth # 2: *My life story is insignificant because I haven't been through anything very traumatic or dramatic.*

Some live with the myth that pain is only caused by dramatic circumstances. They say they've had a great life and they judge their Heart Shapers as inconsequential compared to others who have had it far worse.

Peter Scazzero says, "Very, very few people emerge from their families of origin emotionally whole or mature. In my early years of ministry, I believed the power of Christ could break my curse, so I barely gave any thought to how the home I'd left long ago might still be shaping me. After all, didn't Paul teach in 2 Corinthians 5:17 that when you become a Christian, old things pass away and all things become new? But crisis taught me I had to go back and understand what these old things were in order for them to begin to pass away."

Pain can be intense when you feel betrayed, mistreated, abandoned, or rejected. But pain can be subtle, like the moments when someone isn't listening to you or you feel misunderstood. The repetition of these kinds of subtle jabs has a cumulative impact on us. Subtle or great, pain is more common than many of us want to admit, and pain grabs hold of the pen and writes things that don't belong in our stories.

Maybe the painful influences are obvious: You've been abused. You've been through a nasty divorce. You lost a child way too early. You grew up in an alcoholic home. You're an addict. You live with someone with a personality disorder. The list is endless. You may not want to admit how much your pain has shaped your life, but it's obvious to everyone else.

But for some, the pain isn't as obvious. Your heart might have been shaped by a thousand little things over time instead of one big blow. Not getting a date with your first love might have shaped your sensitive teenage heart. When someone made fun of you again and again, there were no bruises or blood, but it hurt almost as bad as a person being beaten by a family member. The experience of pain isn't always determined by the degree of drama that accompanies it, but none of it is inconsequential.

And if you've come from a good family and had few hardships, you might be under the false assumption that you have been spared from the influences of an imperfect life, but you're almost certainly wrong.

When Ken showed up to Blessing Ranch and was asked to tell his story, he said, "It won't take long." He shared in a few sentences about how he came from a Christian family, went to church for as long as he could remember, and had been happily married for 16 years. Ken needed his eyes opened to the sneaky, painful influences that made their way into his heart. Ken was very insecure. He knew that much, but he had no idea that even a loving family could leave him feeling like he didn't measure up. His parents were full of praise, which he understood as full acceptance. He didn't realize that the encouragement only came when he had done something well. The time he won the basketball game with a last-second shot and the times he made the honor roll were the only times the praise came. He thought that was love, but it left him feeling desperate and empty. As a result, he spent his life feeling like he was one move away from losing people's approval, and he had been working himself into the ground trying to perform well enough to be recognized as worthy. He'd completely discounted the significance of his Heart Shapers.

If you had an amazing childhood and life has been smooth ever since, you may be relatively healthy, but you've still had pain. We are fallen people who live in a fallen world. Things that happened long ago may not consume you now, but even a pebble in your shoe can make you limp. If you don't pay attention to the pebble, you might find yourself saying, "I never saw this coming," or "I never thought this would happen to me."

Dramatic circumstances may have deeper effects that are difficult to undo, but don't dismiss the cumulative power of your Heart Shapers just because your story isn't full of drama, scandal, and trauma. Take your eyes off the absence of the big and dramatic and put them on the subtle, poisonous, and consistent messages your heart might have received.

You don't get to choose most of the people and events that have shaped your story, but you can choose how you deal with them.

Myth # 3: *If I have enough faith, I shouldn't have imperfections in my heart's story.*

A third fallacy is that our faith should have kept us from being damaged. Some can't acknowledge any imperfections in their heart's story because they believe it would be an indictment against the strength of their faith. They fear that if they acknowledge someone or something has had more influence than God, it might mean their relationship with Him is inauthentic.

It may be true that pain gets in the way of exercising your faith from time to time. Perhaps it holds you back from trusting God or surrendering full control to Him, even though you firmly believe in the principles of trust and surrender. Pain has such shaping power that it can write things on your heart that are inconsistent with your faith, such as fear, control, bitterness, self-pity, and self-sufficiency. The reality of these internal flaws leaves you feeling like a fraud. In fact, it may be so uncomfortable that you try to ignore these perceptions.

The internal conflict doesn't mean your faith is a fraud. It means your heart doesn't always cooperate with your faith. Your heart's story may scream that God doesn't love you and that your life doesn't count, but you know better. Hold your head up as a believer and acknowledge that pain has had shaping power in your life. And know this: You're not the only one. All of us wrestle with the inner conflict between our pain and our faith, even the most faithful among us, and even those who won't admit it.

God isn't shaking His finger at you in judgment because you wrestle with fear and doubt. He's lovingly calling you into the process of redemption, truth, and healing.

Actually, those who have great faith have the courage to be ruthlessly honest—with God, with themselves, and with at least one other person—about their internal battles.

Myth #4: We simply can't know what God is up to.

Over the years, we've talked with men and women who have given up on a rich, real connection with God—and these are Christian leaders. At least for some of them, their doubts were formed years ago when they trusted God for a big ask, but God didn't answer the way they had hoped or—more importantly—the way they'd expected. Whether it was one big disappointment or many smaller ones rolled together, they concluded that it's safer to give up on God than to expect intimacy with Him.

If we don't expect God to meet us in our pain and show us His presence in it, we avoid it at all costs. Likewise, if we don't expect to be able to trust God when we can't understand Him, we won't be very eager to examine pieces of our past that can't be healed by logic.

In the Scriptures, we find two seemingly opposing passages, and they're written by the same person. In 1 Corinthians, Paul assures them, "But we have the mind of Christ." This infers that our thoughts can be, to some degree, correlated with Christ's thoughts. But before this statement in the same verse it says, "For who has known the mind of the Lord, so as to instruct him?" And in Romans after Paul's expansive explanation of God's sovereign plans, he writes, "Who has known the mind of the Lord? Or who has been his counselor?" Both passages are quoted from Isaiah 40.

But the question remains, can we know what God is up to? When we believe we have no way of knowing what God is up to, we see no point in going back to the past. With this perspective, the only choice is to live with it. We're afraid that going back into past hurts that just don't seem to make sense (like being cheated on when you were nothing but faithful or when your dad died of cancer even though he was such a good person) might be left irreconcilable and dredge up even more unwanted pain. This perspective makes the past irrelevant.

When we sense God telling us something, can we be absolutely sure it's God speaking? The counsel of Scripture tells us that God speaks through His Word, giving light, hope, and direction. We can certainly know something of the heart of God through the covenants, and especially, through the sacrifice of Christ. And the Spirit speaks to our hearts. Sometimes, the direction God gives seems crystal clear, but many times, it remains, at least in part, mysterious. The fact that God doesn't give us detailed information with concrete assurances isn't a cause for alarm. He is infinitely wiser, infinitely more loving, and infinitely more powerful than anything we can imagine—and He delights to share His heart with us.

So, the answer is, "No, we can't know everything because we're not God," but "Yes, he speaks to us through the Word and through the still small voice of the Spirit." He knows, even when we don't. We need to trust more in Him than in our ability to know what He's up to. That means we can face our past with confidence that God has walked through it with us, and He reminds us of His trustworthiness as we acknowledge things that can't be reconciled to our logic.

Myth #5: If I really trust God, there's really no need to examine my past.

If I really trust God, shouldn't that mean He'll take care of it, and I don't have to? Some people think exercising trust means they can avoid the unhealed parts of themselves. That's not trust; that's denial. Trusting God means meeting God in the middle of the unwelcome parts of our stories and giving Him access to do the real healing that happens in the depths of our hearts.

Others fear that they'll just become self-absorbed if they dive into their story and pay attention to their pain. It goes against their theology that says, "You're supposed to die to yourself!" But self-absorption isn't the result of self-examination. Actually, the opposite is true. As you face your pain and grow through it, your attention moves away from yourself.

Myth #6: If I really trust God with my past, I'll become weird and people will laugh at me.

This is another way to dismiss the power of objectivity. Some of us don't want to depend too much on God because we've seen the crazy things some believers have said and done, and they ascribed their odd behavior to God's leading. We can use their strangeness as an excuse to back away from God, but it would be a big mistake. Trusting God doesn't make us weird; trusting Him makes us wise. Certainly, this wisdom sometimes (often?) is countercultural. When we forgive those who offend us, speak up for those who have no voice, and care for those who have nothing to offer us, we can be considered strange to people who don't know the heart of Christ. If that's weird, count us in.

Your Vulnerability

As you come face-to-face with the reality that more than God has shaped your heart, give yourself plenty of grace. To help you do that, consider a few of the reasons why Heart Shapers have such power, leaving you vulnerable to their influences, even if you've tried to forget or move on for years.

1) *Negative Heart Shapers are tangible*.

Life is tangible. But God isn't.

The problem is that what we see, what we hear, and what other people do often make more sense to our hearts than what we read in the pages of the Bible. Experiences are palpable.

For example, even though you may know that God says you are valuable, it's very hard to ignore the many times your mom told you, "You're worthless!" The idea that God loves you may not seem as real as the condescending tone in her voice and the powerful echoes of her stinging words.

Others' words ring in your ears for years, and you can still see the disgusted look on the person's face and remember details like the scent of the room. The moment is burned into your memory, and it feels more real than a thousand passages of Scripture about God's amazing love.

2) *Repeated wounds can't be ignored.*

When pain happens again and again, you gather mounting evidence to prove the flawed and destructive messages. In other words, if you hear the same message enough, you start to believe it—and the message is both spoken and unspoken. The daughter of an uninvolved father gets the message that she's not worth his time. She then marries a top-level executive who seems more interested in being successful at work than spending time with her, despite her frequently obvious (and not-so-obvious) pleas for attention. As she spends years feeling discounted in her marriage, she's more convinced than ever that she's not worth anyone's time. It may seem like she had no chance of escaping this ultimate conclusion given the constant repetition and reinforcement of the message: "You aren't worth it."

The pain is so intense that you may minimize it ("It wasn't that bad."), excuse it ("She couldn't help it."), or deny it ("I don't know what you're talking about."). The truth makes us feel even more vulnerable, and we crave safety—even the safety of a lie. For instance, victims of abuse often insist the violence is their fault. An alcoholic believes he can quit any time he wants, and he refuses to listen to his family's complaints that he's ruining his life and theirs. For him, safety is found in denial and another bottle.

For some, a single tragic moment traumatizes them, but for many, a thousand paper cuts of criticism gradually crush their spirits. The cumulative power of repeated pain leaves an almost unreadable story on your heart.

3) *Sometimes, it takes only one.*

A 2001 article called "Bad is Stronger Than Good" reports, "Bad emotions, bad parents and bad feedback have more impact than good ones. Bad impressions and bad stereotypes are quicker to form and more resistant to disconfirmation than good ones." Have you ever noticed that it takes multiple compliments to overcome the impact of one criticism?

If an experience is traumatic or grips your heart intensely, sometimes it only takes one moment to tip the scale and edit your heart's story. Think of a child who's grown up in a loving home that's full of stability and safety. Her parents love her and protect her, so she sees God as her protector, too. But a trusted family friend molests her while he's watching her one day. Her heart's story is edited in an instant. The years of safety and assurance are ripped away and replaced with fear. Suddenly, she feels out of control. It doesn't matter that is the *one* time she wasn't protected. It doesn't matter that her parents, friends, and church family would never hurt her. She now has fear written in the deepest places in her heart. Now, she sees God as distant and the world as a threat.

Some of us have been relatively protected from trauma and heartache, *but* even one experience, if painful enough, can invalidate all that. Some of the traumas people have shared with us include sexual abuse, physical abuse, being the victim of a crime, a family member brutally murdered, post-traumatic stress from being in war, and similar events. Even the everyday experiences of life can change your heart in an instant. Remember my (John's) story from Chapter 1? In one moment of sheer embarrassment at school as a young kid, my heart was changed for decades when I concluded I was stupid. Whether seemingly big or small to the outside observer, the heart can latch on to meaning that shifts the trajectory of your life. And once the pain is written upon your heart, it's not easy to undo the changes it has made.

Competing Influences

The story of your heart begins to take shape early in your life. The Heart Shapers you experienced as a young person have a great deal of influence over your story. In fact, many experts say that the trajectory of our emotional life is shaped in the first three years of life.

As we grow up, we continually encounter Heart Shapers—those that communicate love and value, and messages that challenge what we desperately need to hear. Throughout this process, we aren't objective. We more readily absorb the messages that confirm previous statements that we're unsafe and unloved. And our hearts resist messages that feel unfamiliar, even the most positive ones.

We're asking you to walk through the process of redeeming the story of your heart. No matter how the Heart Shapers have deceived you, God is stepping in to give you alternatives—new, powerfully positive messages and experiences. But be ready for a fight. The old doesn't give up easily.

You're not alone in the fight. The Holy Spirit is your advocate, like a defense attorney who defends you against the prosecutor's attacks. The Holy Spirit is the change agent. He uses the inherent power of God's Word and the comfort expressed by wise believers to transform you from the inside out. Gradually, you believe the Father's statement to Jesus is also His word to you: "You are my Son, whom I love; with you I am well pleased" (Mark 1:11).

Your Heart Shapers

As you identify your Heart Shapers, you'll have to look backward before you can look forward. And you'll have to look beneath the events of the past to see their impact.

Rid yourself of any myths. Say "no" to any guilt that tells you that you are judging other people if you acknowledge the negative impact of their behavior or words. Remember that this process is about understanding, not judging. It's okay to acknowledge that your parents weren't perfect. It's okay to name the hurtful things others have done to you. Some of us have suffered from genuine evil and cruelty, but for most of us, the saying is true: "Our parents were doing the best that they knew how to do." And it's okay to admit that you've hurt people, too.

When some people start this process, their existing feelings of shame and defectiveness multiply. They feel even more unworthy, more flawed, and more hopeless. If that's true for you, be honest with God and ask Him to do a powerful and tender work to assure you of His unending love.

In the next few chapters, you'll take the next steps in uncovering and telling the story of your heart.

Reflection

As you look at the ten categories of Heart Shapers listed below, circle three that have had the biggest impact on you.

1) *Life Experiences*: A series of everyday life moments that don't stand out but accumulate into something that matters to your heart.

2) *Family*: The lessons, patterns, and impacts derived from the family of origin.

3) *Defining Moments*: Single events that have extremely strong impact for good or bad. These can include God moments and mountaintop experiences as well as traumatic events.

4) *Biology*: Your nature, personality, physical characteristics, and DNA.

5) *Sin/Evil*: Your sin, others' sin, spiritual warfare.

6) *The Mind*: The way you think, understand, process, and perceive the world around you.

7) *Beliefs*: Your spiritual convictions, guiding principles, moral compass, and anchor points that direct you.

8) *The Emerging Self Concept*: What you learn about who you are, how you see yourself, and your emerging view of self.

9) *Emotions*: Feelings and passions, the affective side of us, how our feelings attach meaning to life.

10) *The Will*: Volition, desires, choices, the logical side of us that attaches meaning.

Now, describe the influence of each of the three.

Look for themes among your top three Heart Shapers. What do they have in common? Did they affect you in similar ways? Explain your answer.

In your partnership with God, what in this chapter is His responsibility, and what is yours?

CHAPTER 3

Sore Spots

So if my behavior contradicts my desires to do good, I must conclude that it's not my true identity doing it, but the unwelcome intruder of sin hindering me from being who I really am.

—ROMANS 7:20 (TPT)

Sore Spots

Heart Shapers

Heart Logic

Private Conclusions

Life Outcomes

Life Lessons

"Why Do I Keep Doing This?"

When Carina walked through our doors, it was apparent she was deeply discouraged. She kept self-sabotaging, putting up roadblocks and finding excuses that kept her from the two things she wanted most—to start a nonprofit and to get married.

Her dream for years had been to start an organization for at-risk kids. Her love and compassion were just waiting to be expressed, but all she did was dream about it. She felt quite clearly that God wanted her to do it, but whenever she let herself dream, all she could see were the risks, and they seemed too daunting to overcome.

Carina had been close to getting married a couple of times, but at 43 she had concluded it probably wasn't going to happen. Every time things started feeling serious with someone, a warning bell started going off in her head, telling her that it was time to break it off. Carina couldn't trust that a loving, supportive man was in her future.

Her life was dominated by a nagging fear. It certainly wasn't the life of strength and beauty beyond description God envisioned for her.

Even so, Carina was successful in many ways. She had joined her dad's sales company and was doing very well. She was a valuable volunteer in the student ministry at her church, and her faith was strong. She wasn't completely paralyzed, but there was something that she couldn't put her finger on, an X factor that prevented her from taking action unless she had ironclad guarantees.

She cringed each time she saw herself back away from the things she wanted. The X factor felt like a wave sweeping over her, leaving her feeling powerless and frustrated.

As she explained her struggle, she kept saying, "I don't know why I keep running away." As Carina unpacked the story of her heart, she began to understand. She had a Sore Spot that had been formed by her Heart Shapers. Her Sore Spot was filled with fear. That was the X factor that kept standing in her way.

Sore Spots

When you experience Heart Shapers that don't reflect God's love, wisdom, and strength, they hurt, and they leave bruises on your heart we call Sore Spots. A Sore Spot is the site of your wound, the place where pain has made a home. When a Sore Spot is formed, your heart's story is altered, deviating from God's gracious intentions.

Carina had experienced some important Heart Shapers. Her parents never divorced, but they fought viciously and split up several times as she was growing up. She lived in fear that her dad would leave for good. She also watched her dad lose a lot of money on some bad investments. Her mother developed a "scarcity mentality" about money, holding tight to every dollar.

These everyday experiences in Carina's life shaped a Sore Spot of fear that created doubt. She expected the worst any time there was uncertainty. When the risks got too great, Carina's Sore Spot overwhelmed her, and she ran. She wasn't filtering things through security and trust as God intended. Instead, her filter was fear, and it paralyzed her.

In the face of unknowns, all Carina could see were the risks, and she felt powerless to change. Her Sore Spot kept out the essential thing that God wanted in her heart: a sense of safety. The absence of safety limited her ability to trust herself to not mess things up, trust other people to keep their word, and trust God with the outcomes in her life.

In our conversations, Carina came face-to-face with the Sore Spot of fear that had been created by her Heart Shapers. As she looked back, she saw the power of her family background to create the Sore Spot. With this insight, her life made much more sense. She finally had a name to put to the X factor, and now she could bring it into the light to be challenged, redeemed, and healed.

Pain Marks the Spot

Pain writes the words of your Sore Spots. Those words become the unseen and unwanted force that creates a perceptual bias (that is, a conviction without evaluation) that determines your goals, your ability to give and receive love, your capacity to take risks, and so much more.

—Six Common Sore Spots

In our conversations with people over many years, we've seen the same Sore Spots over and over again. They surface in six primary ways:

- *Shame:* Feelings of overwhelming guilt or embarrassment, or believing you deserve blame. Shame causes you to see things that go wrong as your fault and incites self-condemnation.
- *Fear:* Feeling out of control or unprotected; experiencing undue worry and pervasive anxiety. Fear leads you to consistently expect the worst and want to protect yourself.
- *Inadequacy/Insecurity:* Feeling like you're not enough or that you don't measure up. Feelings of inadequacy and insecurity

cause you to doubt your abilities. They make you believe
others are condemning you or are disappointed in you.

- *A sense of rejection:* Feeling like you don't belong and aren't
  wanted. You see yourself as expendable, cast aside, or
  dismissed.
- *Feeling unvalued:* Feeling unimportant, forgotten, or unworthy.
  This perception causes you to feel minimized, overlooked,
  and despised. It creates self-perceptions of inferiority and
  insignificance.
- *Pride:* Feeling superior to others or being overly self-focused.
  Pride makes you see only success in yourself and failure in
  others. It inflates your importance and exaggerates your
  perception of others' admiration for you.

These may or may not be words you typically use to describe
yourself. For many, these Sore Spots remain unnamed and covered
up by secondary or surface level emotions like frustration, anger, or
disappointment. You have to strip away your defenses and dig down
to the roots of your heart to actually see a Sore Spot.

A Sore Spot might feel really painful and tender. The pain might
be fresh and real, but it might not feel very sore at all, perhaps numbed
by the passing of time or being distracted so you don't have to pay
attention. A good indication of an unrecognized Sore Spot is a "dis-
proportional emotional response" to a person or situation—either too
much or too little. Too much is when someone blows up in anger
or craters in tears at a relatively minor event; too little is the lack of
normal, healthy emotions. In these cases, someone has numbed out to
avoid the discomfort of the Sore Spot.

As we've seen, pain leaves an impact, whether it came through one traumatic moment or a thousand little moments. Even an old bruise that has lost its sensitivity is still a sign of pain. When she came to see us, Carina wouldn't have said that her parents' tumultuous marriage or her dad's bad financial choices were things that bothered her. She didn't feel consumed by these things every day, yet they had written fear into her heart's story instead of safety and trust.

The Unseen and Unwanted Force

Last week I (Charity) picked up an apple that had been sitting on my kitchen counter for a couple weeks. I noticed that a bruise had developed on one side. I don't like wasting things, so I picked it up to take a bite, assuming I could avoid the bruised part. I expected the sweetness of a Honeycrisp apple, but it was bitter! The taste of the entire apple was affected by the bruise. That's what Sore Spots can do to us. Even a small bruise in your heart can influence the flavor of much of your life.

At some point, you've probably been where Carina was—utterly frustrated with yourself for not being able to get beyond a repeated behavior, thought, or feeling. You *feel* stuck because you *are* stuck. How many times have you asked yourself these questions: "Why do I keep doing this?" "Why do I keep holding back when I really want to be more connected to people?" "Why do I avoid applying for a new job when I can't stand what I'm doing?" "Why do I keep working too much even though I'm so tired all the time?" "Why do I feel like I have to control everything all the time?"

Are we all just crazy? No, we have Sore Spots in our hearts which have significantly shaped the storylines of our lives. Every moment of every day, our Sore Spots drive us or inhibit us, almost certainly more than we realize.

The Filter

My (Charity's) husband spent a summer years ago working as an interpretive guide at Rocky Mountain National Park in Colorado. He guided visitors through the park and helped them see it through a new lens. He showed them how to see the wildlife, the plants, the birds, and the terrain in a way their city-trained eyes couldn't see. What looked like a bunch of dead trees was actually the home to woodpeckers and other birds. What used to look like big cows were majestic elk. And what used to look like an ordinary pond was an intricately developed ecosystem beavers had created to ingeniously raise their young, protect themselves from predators, and store food for the winter. My husband changed the way the visitors saw the park and brought a new beauty to their experience.

When there's an unredeemed Sore Spot reigning in your heart, it will be your interpretive guide. It will tell you how to see things, what to believe, and even what to do. But instead of displaying beauty, it will steal beauty from your life.

In Carina's experience, situations that were filled with risks and unknowns were viewed through the filter of her Sore Spot of fear. In fact, fear was the lens she saw everything through, putting her focus on potential problems, what could go wrong, and the likelihood of bad endings.

Unredeemed Sore Spots filter your life in three main ways: the way you think, the way you feel, and the way you act.

—Filtering the Way You Think

Have you ever used photo filters on your smartphone? Maybe you wanted to make yourself look a little better. Maybe you wanted to enhance the beauty of a sunset by bringing out the vibrancy of the oranges and pinks in the sky. Or maybe you just wanted to be a better photographer with a little extra help from filters.

Filters can turn photos black and white, transform the color to cool or warm shades, and even make them look like comic art. Some filters are quite dramatic and leave the original photo almost unrecognizable. Others slightly adjust the photo, leaving most of the original image intact.

Just as filters affect your perceptions of photos, Sore Spots affect how you see yourself, other people, God, and the world around you. They can distort everything you perceive, coloring it with the pain (whether actively felt or not) that defines the Sore Spot.

Your Sore Spot can affect your ability to see things the way God does. You may have known God's truths, but your thoughts and emotions may mirror your Sore Spot more than the truth you know. You may see risk where God sees trust. You might see "I can't" when God sees "You can." You might see only your shame and defectiveness when God sees the compassion in your heart.

Your Sore Spot creates a confirmation bias, so you see only what you're looking for, not what's really there. You interpret new information as evidence of what you already think or believe. Your filter has a seemingly magnetic energy that attracts what fits the Sore Spot and rejects what doesn't!

For instance, if your Sore Spot is rejection, it seems that rejection is waiting around every corner. If your Sore Spot is insecurity, it seems that everyone is judging you and accusing you of doing a terrible job. Or if your Sore Spot is fear, you'll see threats everywhere. When your heart filters life through the Sore Spot, you don't (and can't) see things as they really are.

Ten men who traveled to the Land of Canaan over 3000 years ago may have seen the land filtered through their collective Sore Spot. In Numbers 13 and 14, we read the story of 12 scouts who were sent by Moses to explore Canaan, the land promised to the Israelites, and bring back their observations. Moses wanted to know what they were up against as they prepared to take the land. He wanted to know whether the people there were strong or weak, whether the land was fertile or poor, and if the land was protected or unprotected (Numbers 13:17-20).

The 12 scouts reported back to Moses after 40 days. Based on the conflicting stories, you'd think he had split the scouts, sending them in two different directions. Two of the scouts, Joshua and Caleb, reported that Canaan was a "rich land flowing with milk and honey" (v. 8b). They said of the people of Canaan, "They are only helpless prey to us! They have no protection, but the Lord is with us! Don't be afraid of them!" (v. 9b) Joshua and Caleb saw promise, hope, and victory.

But the other 10 scouts saw doom and defeat. Their picture wasn't just one shade off; it was completely contrary to what Joshua and Caleb had seen! The 10 reported, "The land we traveled through and explored will devour anyone who goes to live there. All the people we saw were huge. We even saw giants there, the descendants of Anak. Next to them we felt like grasshoppers, and that's what they thought, too!" (v. 32b-33)

All 12 had seen the same things. How could some see an easy victory while others saw giants? How could some see milk and honey while others saw a land that promised to devour them?

This wasn't just a case of optimism versus pessimism. This wasn't just Caleb and Joshua looking on the bright side while the others were realistic. Something was empowering the lens of the 10 scouts: the unseen impact of a Sore Spot.

The scouts who saw doom may have shared a Sore Spot filtering their perspective. Remember what they'd been through: They'd been slaves their whole lives! Maybe their enslavement had created a Sore Spot of helplessness. Imagine the impact of having no control, being overpowered, and constantly being a victim. Perhaps slavery had left them with defeat and "we can't" written on their hearts. As they looked out on the Land of Canaan, helplessness may have been their filter. That's why they saw normal people as giants, and their misperception made them feel small and vulnerable like grasshoppers.

What about Joshua and Caleb? Surely slavery had taken its toll on their hearts, too. Either they made it through slavery without a Sore Spot purely by the grace of God or they'd already redeemed their Sore Spot with God's help. As they looked out over the land, their hearts were running on God's story, which gave them trust and hope in God rather than hopelessness and defeat from their lives as slaves. As they saw Canaan through God's perspective, they were able to see the potential, the possibility, and the promise of the land God was giving them. To Joshua and Caleb, it looked like the land of milk and honey, because it was.

—Filtering the Way You Feel

The role of emotions in filtering our present experiences is two-fold:

First, think about these words that describe common Sore Spots: shame, fear, inadequacy, rejection, worthlessness, pride. These words are charged with emotion because they're connected to deep pain. Some carry an intense loneliness, and others are attached to anxiety and depression. Sore Spots are usually full of emotion, and the intensity of emotion can lock you into biased narratives, lead you to misinterpret others' hearts, and cause you to receive the wrong feedback from others.

Before going any farther, it's important to remind the logical and analytical people that the presence of a Sore Spot isn't always correlated with intense, out-of-control emotions. For some, the experience of a Sore Spot is more cognitive than affective. Nevertheless, the Sore Spot's influence remains, even when high emotions aren't involved.

On the other hand, many people say, "If I feel it, it's true. You have no right to challenge me." They dig in their heels because their feelings make whatever they perceive seem completely legitimate. Because the Sore Spot is so convincing, feelings are accepted without evaluation as the beacon of truth. Our emotions aren't right or wrong—they simply are. But they're important because they signal what's going on in our hearts, like a flashing light on the dashboard of our cars. We're wise to pay attention.

Emotions insert themselves into the filtering process in a second way: Painful emotions validate and reinforce our flawed perception, which then circles back to affirm the painful emotions. We get more afraid, angrier, and more discouraged. Or we become numb in an attempt to avoid the pain.

When we look closely at the 10 spies in Numbers 13 and 14, we see how their Sore Spots may have filtered their emotions as they viewed the Land of Canaan. If it's true that the slave life they'd experienced left them with fear and defeat as Sore Spots, they would have been overwhelmed with more fear and defeat as they looked at the land and the people. A sense of helplessness could have caused them to feel incapable, perhaps convincing them the land would "devour" them (v. 32b). That was certainly a declaration of helplessness!

But Joshua and Caleb must have had something quite different written on their hearts. If trust and hope were written there, excitement and possibility were the feelings shaping what they saw in Canaan. Their confidence gave them eyes to see "a rich land flowing with milk and honey" (v. 8b). They were ready to go!

—Filtering the Way You Act

You experience a cascade from the way you think and feel to the way you act. The cloudy perspective that your Sore Spot gives you, coupled with the physiological activation and subjective experience of emotion, takes you off course, and you make unwise decisions. You skip a critical step of evaluation: "Should I listen to myself?" Without considering that your heart has misguided you, you let the dominant message from your Sore Spot propel you into action.

When Sore Spots take over part of God's intended story, God's truth is stuck in your head as knowledge. It can't live in your heart where it shapes good and godly actions. As always, you act according to what's written on your heart.

It's a safe bet that the 10 scouts' Sore Spot told them to go home. That wasn't God's plan. And Caleb didn't listen to them. He was a man of action. He insisted, "Let's go at once to take the land. We can certainly conquer it!" (Numbers 13:30b) Caleb and Joshua were ready to charge ahead with God's plan for action because they didn't have hopelessness and defeat written on their hearts. Even if they had moments of doubt, hope and victory were able to dominate.

Erin was a power-house leader, at least as measured by the results she produced. Her goal was for her team to outperform every other team—and itself—every quarter, and it did. But people didn't like working for her. She treated them like tools she used to get results. They weren't willing to hang in much longer in the environment she had created.

Something was written on Erin's heart that was shaping the way she led, but she didn't understand it yet.

When Erin walked into her office every day, all she could see was what was undone and unfinished. She saw people who were lingering in conversation and wasting valuable time. She saw long, collaborative meetings as counter-productive. Of course, her leadership style was built on these perspectives. She kept the agenda of meetings strictly business and shut people down if they started brainstorming new ideas. Erin prided herself on being direct because it was the fastest way to achieve results. She didn't beat around the bush or soften things for the sake of others' feelings. To her, pushing someone to get things done faster was a much better model of leadership than taking the time to make someone feel appreciated. She was intentional about not letting personal feelings or the needs of others get in the way of "good business decisions." While she was making great things happen for the business, she didn't realize that she was leaving a wake of devastation behind her.

After a 360° review, she was prompted to ask herself a question: "Why do people feel so run over and unvalued by me?" It was a confusing question to her. She had been living the last several years with intense pride in her leadership.

After humbling herself enough to listen to more feedback, she began to realize there was something in her that was skewing her view of good leadership and shaping the results-driven way she led. Erin began to see inadequacy written on her heart, and it made her see results as the most prized possession. Her Sore Spot had everything to do with how she led. When she got her team to win (as measured by results), it kept her from the uncomfortable feeling that she wasn't enough (her Sore Spot of inadequacy). She craved the few moments of relief, power, and satisfaction every time the team achieved a higher level of performance.

Maybe you drink excessively because your Sore Spot of defeat tells you there's no hope and there's no point. Maybe you're critical of your spouse because your Sore Spot of rejection tells you that your spouse doesn't value you at all, and your harsh words are a form of revenge. Maybe you push past your limits because your Sore Spot of inadequacy tells you that your performance gives you value. Maybe you stopped going to church because your Sore Spot of shame convinced you that everyone is judging you for the mistake you made.

Almost certainly, your Sore Spot compels you to make choices that you don't want to make. It creates a glass ceiling that limits your ability to take the next step. Your Sore Spot keeps you from fully living out the purposes of God.

The Avoidance of Pain

Why do your Sore Spots have so much influence? Because you're highly motivated to keep from experiencing any more pain. Even if you don't remember the pain, your heart does—and it wants nothing more than to protect itself from feeling any more rejection, shame, fear, or other kind of pain. The Sore Spot tells you exactly what to do to defend yourself against potential pain so you can remain safe and comfortable.

Think about how it feels when someone squeezes a bruise on your arm. It hurts! You react immediately by pulling back or swatting the other person's hand away. That's what happens when something hits your Sore Spot. It's uncomfortable—no, it's painful. Your natural instinct is to stop the pain as fast as possible by whatever means it takes in your thoughts, feelings, and actions. And "whatever means" includes unhealthy, unproductive pathways.

Psychologist Greg Lester has studied why it is so difficult for people to change, and he concluded that over many years, we've constructed a powerful network of emotions, beliefs, and assumptions that tell us, "Life has to be this way." Even when we receive new information, and we're sure the information is true and promises relief, hope, and joy, it conflicts with what we believe to be true, and we fiercely resist it. In "Why beliefs are hard to change," Lester observes, "When data and belief come into conflict, the brain does not automatically give preference to data. This is why beliefs—even bad beliefs, irrational beliefs, silly beliefs, or crazy beliefs—often don't die in the face of contradictory evidence. The brain . . . is extremely reticent to jettison its beliefs. Like an old soldier with an old gun who does not quite trust that the war is really over, the brain often refuses to surrender its weapon even though the data say it should."

So, don't be surprised that addressing your Sore Spots looks like a mountain to climb.

The Sore Spot Has Taken Over

Your heart may have been bruised so badly that the Sore Spot has dominion. There's been so much pain that it has consumed your thoughts, feelings, and choices—every aspect of your heart, from corner to corner. There's little room to bypass it, so it influences every aspect of your life.

For instance, someone who is completely consumed by fear always finds one thing to worry about and discounts reassurances. The fearful person imagines the worst case scenario first and has a nagging sense of impending doom. Or it might be someone who can't trust anyone, no matter how much they've proven to be trustworthy. Maybe it's the person who has felt so unvalued that they've given up on people and written them off. Their Sore Spot is exerting influence in most areas of their lives virtually all the time.

Lots of Room Left for God's Beautifully Edited Story

Even if you have a Sore Spot, you probably have a lot of room for parts of God's story to be expressed in you. That's why many people with Sore Spots can still function very well and have noble qualities.

Remember Carina, who was paralyzed by fear? As you saw, not everything in her life was limited by her Sore Spot. She was successful in her job, and she had a strong faith. Despite her fear, she experienced a measure of esteem, belonging, and love.

Carina would have been foolish, though, to let the positive aspects of her life convince her there was no need to deal with her Sore Spot. Even though she was successful in many ways, she couldn't have the things that mattered most to her (starting a nonprofit and marriage) because fear was stopping her.

Sometimes Sore Spots only reveal themselves when life really presses in. Difficult circumstances can strip you of your defenses and expose the Sore Spot.

Don't be fooled that a seemingly put-together life means you don't have a Sore Spot that needs attention. Don't let pockets of health convince you to minimize your Sore Spot and call it a "quirk."

God's new, edited story is worth fighting for because it enables you to be the best spouse, parent, leader, and servant you can be.

Reflection

On a scale of 0 (not at all) to 10 (all day, every day), to what extent have you experienced these Sore Spots?

_____ Shame

_____ Fear

_____ Inadequacy/Insecurity

_____ Fear of rejection

_____ Feeling unvalued

_____ Pride

For the Sore Spot that scored the highest, how has it filtered:

- How you think?

- How you feel?

- How you act?

What are some ways your Sore Spot has "taken over"?

What difference do you think it will make if you trust God to heal your Sore Spot?

What steps do you need to take in your partnership with God, and what are steps only He can take?

CHAPTER 4

Sore Spots as the
Source of Genius

Now, with God's help, I shall become myself.

—SØREN KIERKEGAARD

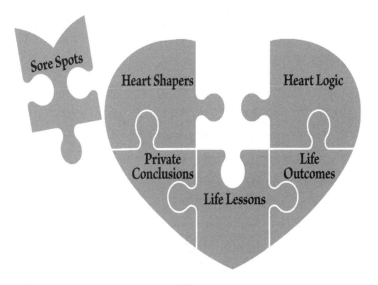

A wise seminary professor commented to his students: "The problems you suffer during the first half of your life become the source of your impact for the rest of your life." We agree, and we say it this way: "Your Sore Spots can become the source of your genius."

The disciple Peter had a Sore Spot. He was the first called to become a disciple of Christ. He dropped everything, including his career as a fisherman, to follow Jesus. He was part of Jesus' inner circle and showed how sold-out he was through these words, "Even if I have to die with you, I will never disown you" (Matthew 26:35).

But when pressure came, Peter caved. He denied knowing Jesus—his leader, his teacher, his Savior, his friend. When Jesus was arrested, we can only imagine the fear that rose up in Peter. The Gospels tell us that Peter reacted by grabbing a sword and taking a swipe at one of the men who had come to arrest Jesus. Thankfully, the fisherman wasn't too skilled with a sword. He cut off the man's ear. Jesus reminded Peter why He had come, and He reattached the man's ear. When Jesus was taken for a trial before the Jewish council, Peter went along and waited outside. Several people asked him if he was one of Jesus' followers, but Peter realized that if they were going to kill Jesus, they were going to kill His followers, too! His instinct was to protect himself by lying. As Peter was questioned about his relationship with Jesus, he denied knowing Him, not once but three times—all before the rooster crowed, just as Jesus had predicted (John 18:15-27).

When Peter realized what he'd done, his heart sank. A sold-out, committed disciple of Jesus had rejected Him out of raw fear.

Peter undoubtedly meant it when he told Jesus earlier, "I will never disown you."

What happened to Peter as a result of that denial? Imagine with us for a moment what could have been. You don't escape moments like that without your heart being terribly bruised. Scripture says that he broke down and wept (Matthew 26:75). Waves of shame washed over him. He may have felt that he'd lost the right to call himself a follower of Jesus. He had such grand plans to reign with Jesus in the new kingdom, but those dreams were shattered. Peter's denial bruised his heart, leaving a Sore Spot of shame.

As we watch Peter's behavior after the denial, it's easy to imagine shame driving his actions. It filtered his self-perception, and it may have led him to give up on himself. In John 21:3, Peter says, "I'm going out to fish." Do you think that Peter's shame caused him to conclude that he was no longer part of Jesus' plans? Perhaps he saw himself as a failure, and he resigned himself to the fact that his time of influence was over. Maybe he was thinking, "All I can be is a fisher of fish, not a fisher of men anymore." Fortunately, that's not the end of the story for Peter.

Jesus transformed Peter's Sore Spot. After Peter's denial and the crucifixion, Jesus appeared to the disciples several times. One of these was when a group of them had gone fishing. After a miracle breakfast, Jesus took Peter aside. John's Gospel takes us to the scene: "When they had finished eating, Jesus said to Simon Peter, 'Simon son of John, do you love me more than these?' 'Yes, Lord,' he said, 'you know that I love you.' Jesus said, 'Feed my lambs.' Again Jesus said, 'Simon son of John, do you love me?' He answered, 'Yes, Lord, you know that I love you.' Jesus said, 'Take care of my sheep.' The third time he said to him, 'Simon son of John, do you love me?' Peter was hurt because Jesus asked him the third time, 'Do you love me?' He said, 'Lord, you know all things; you know that I love you.' Jesus said, 'Feed my sheep'" (John 21:15-17).

Jesus didn't confront Peter with fierce condemnation and words like, "You blew it!" but instead He asked, "Do you love me?" During those three strategic exchanges, Jesus wasn't actually trying to find out whether Peter loved Him. He already knew that. He needed to heal Peter's shame by helping him see that his love for Jesus was still real. When Jesus told Peter, "Feed my sheep," He was trying to get Peter to see that He loved him and still called him worthy. The conversation was about the redemption of shame. Jesus showed Peter that it's not about performance; it's about love. Jesus reminded him that he was still His disciple and a fisher of men.

Without this conversation between Jesus and Peter, we'd have to rewrite the book of Acts. After his Sore Spot was redeemed, we see a very different Peter—humble yet bold. He preached the message on the Day of Pentecost, and 3,000 believed. In Acts 4, Peter and John were confronted by the Sanhedrin and questioned for healing a crippled man. Peter answered, "If we are being called to account today for an act of kindness shown to a man who was lame and are being asked how he was healed, then know this, you and all the people of Israel: It is by the name of Jesus Christ of Nazareth, whom you crucified but whom God raised from the dead, that this man stands before you healed" (Acts 4:9-10). Peter had changed. He was again defined by his God-given identity instead of by his mistakes. He was no longer a shame-filled, discouraged man. He was confident and bold, with security and redemption guiding his heart—ingredients of God's beautiful story.

Peter's shame could have been a threat to the future of the church. What if he had given up on his apostolic calling? Jesus dissolved his shame in the experience of love and security. That's how Peter could be a major force in establishing the church! Ironically, Peter's wound became the source of his usefulness, his impact, his genius.

Like Peter, the site of your wound can become the source of your genius—the very best of you. If we let God heal us and restore us, our Sore Spot will become our strongest point. We'll have more wisdom because we've seen God work when we were hopeless, we'll have more compassion because we've experienced the depths of His grace, and we'll have more strength because the Spirit's power has replaced our weakness. When God has worked, we can look back at the hardest times in our lives with gratitude. Paul wrote, "We also glory in our sufferings, because we know that suffering produces perseverance; perseverance, character; and character, hope" (Romans 5:3b-4).

When your Sore Spot is faced and healed, you're released from the bondage of mediocrity, the paralysis of pain, and artificial limitations. You find yourself with a newfound depth to your spiritual and emotional maturity, filled with greater compassion, humility, love, and faith in God's power that couldn't have been produced any other way.

God not only uses the site of your wound to bring out greatness in you but also through you. In a remarkable admission, the apostle Paul wrote that at one point he "despaired even of life." But God met him there, and he responded, "Praise be to the God and Father of our Lord Jesus Christ, the Father of compassion and the God of all comfort, who comforts us in all our troubles, so that we can comfort those in any trouble with the comfort we ourselves receive from God" (2 Corinthians 1:3-4).

When God meets us in our darkest places to comfort and strengthen us, He prepares us to touch other broken people with His love. If someone knows what it's like to be abandoned and alone, God's healing touch will make that person very sensitive to others' need for belonging. The healed person might be the only one to notice someone feeling uncomfortable and out of place at church and say, "Hi, I'm glad you're here." Those few and simple words have incredible healing power. The compassion we've gained from the redemption of our Sore Spots gives us the capacity to breathe life into the hearts of others. It helps us notice what others may miss. It gives us the conviction to act when others ignore a need or don't even notice it. And it gives us the ability to know just what to say to comfort the person's particular pain.

Healing Your Sore Spot

Pastor and author Tim Keller observes, "Christianity offers not merely a consolation but a restoration—not just of the life we had but of the life we always wanted but never achieved. And because the joy will be even greater for all that evil, this means the final defeat of all those forces that would have destroyed the purpose of God in creation, namely, to live with his people in glory and delight forever."[3] God wants—no, He longs—to edit the story of your heart. The process begins by healing the Sore Spot that has gained power over you.

---

3   Tim Keller, *Walking with God through Pain and Suffering* (New York: Riverhead Books, 2013), p. 159.

Healing your Sore Spot requires revealing the bruises and letting God apply His healing balm of grace, love, and truth. As God touches your pain, your Sore Spot begins to lose its influence. Remember, all of us have experienced pain. Those who enjoy the wonder of God's grace, power, and love have found the courage to partner with God to heal their Sore Spots.

God wants you to trade:

- Shame for righteousness (Romans 5:1)
- Fear for safety (Psalm 16:8, Joshua 1:9)
- Insecurity and inadequacy for God-given esteem (2 Corinthians 3:5, 1 Peter 2:9)
- Rejection for significance (Matthew 18:12)
- Unvalued for cherished (1 John 4:19, John 1:12)
- Pride for humility (Ephesians 4:2, James 4:6, James 4:10)

Will you trust God with your Sore Spot? When you ponder this question, something inside you may be yelling, "Are you crazy? Why would I dredge all that pain up again?" Almost certainly, you'll have to manage an internal civil war between fear and faith. Listen to God call you into the safety of His presence. Listen to Him offering to wrap His loving arms around your heart and place His love where pain once reigned.

Healing the Sore Spot returns a portion of God's original story to your heart, letting His vision for your life more fully return. Your thoughts will begin to sound more like God's. The self-destructive and defensive things you used to do won't make as much sense anymore. Your feelings will become lighter. Your Sore Spot has been a catalyst for the hindrances in your life, but when it's healed, your story can be rewritten.

Becoming aware of Sore Spots isn't about becoming hyper-focused on the pain. It's just the opposite. Acknowledging Sore Spots is a means of healing them, so you can take the focus off them! It's the path to freedom.

Sore Spots as the Source of Genius

We could tell hundreds of wonderful stories of how God has healed Sore Spots and turned them into sources of strength, wisdom, and yes, genius, but we'll focus on these:

SHAME

Gina had a Sore Spot of shame that was rooted in a long series of mistakes as a teenager. She had grown up in the church, but she got sucked into the allure of doing what felt good rather than what she knew she should. She got pregnant at 19 but was grateful she miscarried before she had to choose between an abortion and keeping the baby. She felt intense guilt over the way she had turned her back on her parents and God. She felt so ashamed for becoming pregnant by someone who didn't even care about her. Even when she repented and turned her life around, she couldn't shake the sense of embarrassment. Shame became her identity.

Gina had to heal her Sore Spot. Acknowledging the roots of her shame was incredibly uncomfortable. As she brought the mistakes she'd tried so hard to forget into the light by speaking them to someone else, God took away their power. She was met with grace and nothing else, which gave her a tangible example of God's message for her: She is deeply loved and wonderfully healed. She first had to wrap her head around God's message for her; then she made it personal. Through moments of silence and solitude, she let God speak words of grace directly over her. She then had to break through her resistance to forgive herself for what God had long ago forgiven her.

She walked away with some key messages: She is redeemed from all her bad choices. She is forgiven for her wandering from God. She is covered with grace for the achievements and impact she didn't have but was capable of having. She worked hard to let these new messages have power over her heart by rehearsing them and choosing them daily. She often reminded herself of the sweet moments of silence she spent with God as she let Him speak whispers of grace over her heart. She walked away with a new identity: Righteous.

Gina had felt defective, hopeless, and ruined. As God healed her Sore Spot of shame, she developed enormous compassion for others who struggle with similar wounds. Now, instead of hiding her shame, she uses her healing to help others have hope.

FEAR

Sammy had a Sore Spot of fear. He didn't trust much—maybe not at all. He said he did, and he even thought he did, but he had to always be in complete control of people and situations. He was scared of entrusting outcomes to God, and even more to other people.

Sammy's fear came from his Heart Shapers. A series of deep hurts left him feeling powerless. First was the death of his best friend in a freak drowning accident when they were 10. No one saw it coming. No one could have been prepared. Then his oldest sister developed an addiction to prescription pills when she was 20. The family tried to step in and help, but they couldn't get through to her. As Sammy grew up, he had to sit by and watch as she self-destructed. Then the economy crashed in 2008, leaving Sammy in a really bad spot with some real-estate investments he'd made. With these accumulated wounds, his heart was crippled by fear. He learned to expect the worst, play it safe, and hold the reigns tightly.

Sammy needed to face the pain and grief from the struggles in his life to find freedom from the grip they had on his heart. He had to stop trying to fool others (and himself) that he was a very trusting, relaxed guy. It had all been a façade. Reality hurt, but it was a crucial step. He began to allow God's love to penetrate his defenses, and gradually, he saw that he could trust God far more than he ever imagined. Sammy let go of the façade that all his efforts to protect, control, and prevent were so much less meaningful than God's actual ability to protect (even though that meant bad things might still happen). He also let go of his unrealistic expectations that everything had to turn out perfectly for him to be content. For the first time in his life, Sammy put his heart, his pain, his hopes, and his future into the hands of a loving, wise God. Sammy traded his fear for safety. Sammy's fear had crippled him emotionally and relationally. As God healed his Sore Spot, he could relax in God's love, and he became a bold, confident, yet humble man. Instead of overlooking him, people began to admire him and see him as an example to follow.

INSECURITY/INADEQUACY

Growing up, Maria was constantly compared with her sister. She was the younger one, and nothing she ever did was quite like Laura. Her parents made it clear that she wasn't as pretty, as smart, as funny, or as athletic. When she tried out for the volleyball team, the coach had high expectations for her because Laura had been the top hitter three years before. But Maria wasn't Laura. When the girls brought report cards home, their dad would always praise Laura's A's and give a half-smile to Maria's B+'s. Maria always felt that she was only as good as her last performance—and it was never good enough. Anxiety intensified as she felt more and more pressure to be like her sister.

If Maria had been honest with herself, she would have admitted that many of her failures were only in her mind. After a while, it didn't take others' scowls to tell her that she wasn't measuring up. She became her own harshest critic. Her self-loathing ate away any sense of fulfillment or joy.

Maria had to trade her sense of inadequacy for God-esteem. First, she had to let her heart receive what God said about her performance. She had to see Him smiling at her and telling her, "Well done!" In order to do that, she had to sense God's smile and feel His approval, trusting Him to love and accept her far more than she'd experienced before. She had to accept the fact that God wasn't waiting to love her until she was perfect. She adjusted her concept of God so she could see Him as the loving, affirming God Scripture says He is. She had to give herself permission to be much less than perfect. Finally, she had to disconnect her performance from her worth and rest in the security that she is valued because God treasures her, not because she performed well. In this process, Maria healed her insecurity and replaced it with God-esteem.

As Maria stopped comparing herself to her sister (and everyone else), she was able to share the love of God with others. Her healing became the source of the beautiful twin traits of love and strength.

REJECTION

Emilio had a loving family, but he never felt that he fit in there—or anywhere else. He was always the odd man out. No one seemed to understand his humor, and he took that a sign that no one liked him. He finally found his first close friend in the seventh grade, but soon his friend started hanging out with other boys—and he ditched Emilio. He was left on his own again. His parents' marriage was continually strained, and they divorced when he graduated from high school. Out of her pain, his mom distanced herself from the family, including Emilio. To him, it felt personal. Her rejection was confirmation that his family never really had loved him. After college, he became an engineer and landed his first job. It went well for two years, until budget cuts came when the company downsized. As one of the newest on staff, he was among the first to be let go. He took it very personally as more rejection. He was sure that it wasn't just about seniority. He was convinced people really didn't like working with him.

Emilio's perceptions didn't match reality. People actually liked him, especially when he grew out of those early awkward years. His family didn't reject him nearly as much as it felt. What he couldn't see was how much his parents were struggling behind the scenes in their marriage long before the divorce and how their perpetual conflict created poisonous family dynamics. But Emilio didn't understand all of this, so he assumed their toxic preoccupation with each other meant they didn't care about him. He put walls up to protect himself, and he interpreted every event as an indictment that he wasn't worth knowing. He blamed his boss for laying him off. He couldn't believe that he had only been following HR protocol.

Emilio had to trade his Sore Spot of rejection for significance. He had to examine his cruel judgments of himself, reject them, and embrace God's statement that he is His beloved son, in whom He is well pleased. As part of the process, he began to appreciate his quirkiness as God-given creativity instead of a character flaw. He worked to understand the dynamics going on behind the scenes in his family, and he recognized how his parents' pain affected their messages to him.

Emilio traded his self-rejection for the acceptance of God. He let God remind him how much He pursues him and chooses him. He was finally able to feel significant, first to God. And as he became more secure, he was more open with others. He traded his rejection for significance. Because God had done so much to heal his Sore Spot, Emilio could step into the lives of others who felt unwanted. He reached out to them with the love he experienced in his relationship with God.

UNVALUED

Marcus always believed he didn't matter. He could remember getting on his knees as a kid and begging God for his parents to stop fighting. They didn't. He could remember praying for the girl he liked to like him. She never did. He could remember pleading with God for his uncle to be healed from lung cancer. But he died. Marcus concluded that God really didn't care. He still believed that God was good and sovereign, but He just didn't have any interest in *him*. When Marcus married and they had children, his wife seemed to care far more about their three kids than about him. She gave them all of her energy, both physical and emotional. Marcus dropped hints about things he wanted to do with her, but she either didn't notice or didn't care. Either way, he felt terribly unappreciated and unloved. After his third year of working for a boss who never said "Thank you" or "Good job," he couldn't take it anymore. He became clinically depressed. He wondered how he could be so unlovable that neither his boss, nor his wife, nor even God could take the time to show him that they cared.

Marcus had to rethink his assessment of God's character. He was challenged to remember that God's promise isn't to fix it all, but to walk through the pain and darkness with us (Isaiah 43:2). He spent time in silence and solitude with God in order to feel His presence for the first time in quite a while. A powerful moment occurred when Marcus sat on the beach and realized that God was reminding him that He was there: Someone had written the word "love" in the sand, the waves continually came toward him as if they were pursuing him, and the gorgeous hues of the sunset that night put God's glory on display. Marcus began to see God differently and connected with God's relentless love. About this time, Marcus's eyes were opened about his wife. Instead of seeing her as too busy for him, he realized she was overwhelmed with all the responsibilities of taking care of the children. He saw signs of exhaustion because she was always on "mom duty," longing for permission to let go of a thousand things screaming for her attention. As Marcus gained perception and felt less rejected, he and his wife had some healthy conversations that led them into deeper connection. Though his boss didn't change, the situation became more tolerable because Marcus had a foundation of feeling cherished by God and his wife. His boss's failure to appreciate him didn't have power any longer to take away his sense of value. Marcus traded his Sore Spot of feeling unvalued for knowing he is cherished. His new confidence gave him the motivation to care for others—and the wisdom to know how.

PRIDE

Chelsea was a daddy's girl. They had a special bond that never diminished. It was her dad's mission in life to make Chelsea feel incredibly special, and he didn't disappoint. As beautiful as it appears to have that kind of bond between a dad and daughter, Chelsea was too much of her dad's focus of attention, far outweighing other things that deserved attention, like his marriage. Whatever Chelsea was doing, he was engaged in. Whatever she wanted to talk about, he was interested. Wherever she was going, he was preparing the way. Her dad always thought of her first, and his example taught Chelsea to think of herself first too.

Chelsea knew she was the center of her dad's world, and she expected others to treat her as special. She expected to always be cheered on, never challenged, and for her needs to matter more than anything. Down the road when she married, her husband grew tired of Chelsea's incessant demands—and her pouts or explosions when her demands weren't met.

Chelsea was both crushed and enraged when her husband finally had the guts to call out her pride. She loved Jesus, and until that day, thought her perceptions and behavior were good and right. Gradually, in many conversations with her husband, Chelsea began to see that her pride was dominating her life—and her husband's. She broke down in tears when she realized how much she thought about herself and how little she thought about anyone else. She had lived to be served, not to serve.

To repent of her pride, Chelsea had to swallow a healthy dose of humility. She agreed to meet with a spiritual director who gave her directions, encouragement, and assignments. She started by spending time in awe of God. She sat for hours and contemplated the greatness and goodness of God. She used this time to remember how small she is in comparison to her good and amazing God. She also examined her past, particularly her relationship with her dad, and looked at it through the eyes of God. She saw the unhealthy elevation she'd received from her dad. His behavior had gone beyond love; he had made her his idol, hoping her appreciation for all of his attention would heal the Sore Spot in his own heart. It didn't. Reflecting on the past gave Chelsea a new understanding, and she began to shift her expectations of herself and others.

She spent time writing and reflecting on what it means to be a servant of Christ, and she reoriented her heart to focus on others. She wrote a list of her husband's needs and thought of creative ways to meet them. Chelsea laid down the need to be the focus and traded it for the humility of a true servant. For her, the transformation was stunning. At first, people weren't sure her new attitude was real. After a while, though, they became convinced. They had been guarded and resistant to her, but now she earned a place in their hearts. All of her strengths were filtered and shaped by an amazing new trait: humility.

Follow the Path of Pain

The first step in handing the pen to God and asking Him to edit the story of your heart is to identify your Heart Shapers that created Sore Spots. With this insight, you can take the second step: asking God to heal your Sore Spot. This step asks you to venture into the secret, hidden places of your heart. Though it will feel uncomfortable, find the courage to expose the pain, so it can be healed.

To find your Sore Spot, you have to follow the path of pain. To understand what kind of Sore Spots they have made upon you, look back at the Heart Shapers that have left your heart bruised.

It's often helpful to create a timeline of the significant events in a person's life (see Appendix B, page 303 to create your own).

Heart Shapers: A Life Timeline

Childhood → Adolescence → Early Adulthood → Middle Adulthood → Late Adulthood

As you consider the questions in Appendix B, pay attention to your heart, not your head. Your heart still sees through the eyes of the child who saw her father beat her mother, but her mom never do anything about it, the teenager whose drunk driving cost the life of his best friend, the sister and brother who were tossed back and forth among relatives because their parents were in prison, the hurting five-year-old who felt abandoned, the ten-year-old who was the target of a parent's rage, the seventeen-year-old who wasn't asked to the prom, or the twenty-three-year-old who couldn't get a job. Pain takes all kinds of shapes and comes in all sizes, but all of us have suffered from it. Your heart doesn't see pain through the lens of the present, tempered by the passing of time, age, or denial. Your heart remembers its pain like it happened yesterday. It doesn't lose the muscle memory of the sting, threat, or danger it felt. In order to find your Sore Spot, you have to see pain the way your heart does: fresh and real. Remember that the absence of intense emotions doesn't mean a Sore Spot isn't there.

After seeing all the impacts on your heart, begin to look for the themes. Ask yourself, "What was the cumulative effect of my Heart Shapers on my heart?" This will help you name your Sore Spot(s).

It's much easier to see the path of pain when you have major defining moments. These are the big events that are obviously painful, such as adultery, divorce, abuse, or a serious illness. But the path of pain is subtle and harder to follow when it's made up of more diffuse pain points in everyday life, such as caustic ridicule from a parent or sibling, feeling ongoing irritation from your spouse, having a close friendship unravel, or having trouble keeping up with work demands. We tend to call these things "just part of life"—and they are. But they're also particular points of pain, none of which may seem like a big deal on its own, but when you stack them upon one another, themes emerge and Sore Spots develop. Don't be surprised if you uncover a Sore Spot you didn't anticipate.

The process may sound simple, but it requires the heart of a lion to face hurts we've tried to bury our entire lives. Some people assume they can ask God to "take the pain away." He'll answer that prayer, but probably not like these people hope. A broken leg requires excellent medical care, perhaps surgery, and many months of healing and rehab. That's the way God heals our inner brokenness. The "miracle" is that He brings loving, wise people into our lives to be with us in the process.

Reflection

Which of the six stories about Sore Spots is closest to your experience?

Think back over your life's story. How would it have been different if there were no Sore Spot? What pathways would have looked different in your life? Don't dwell too long in the "what could have beens." Just let that acknowledgment of possibility excite you for what can be.

What help do you need to name and heal your Sore Spot? Who do you trust to step into your life at this moment?

Are you convinced that your Sore Spot needs attention? Why or why not?

What is the strength that God wants to take the place of your Sore Spot? How does God want to minister to your place of pain?

Are you tempted to become passive now that you know your Sore Spot and hope God will instantaneously heal you? What are some reasons God might want you to partner with Him in the healing and transformation?

What are some ways healing our Sore Spots is like healing from a broken leg? Are you willing to go through that process? Explain your answer.

CHAPTER 5

Heart Logic: Unpacking the Four Questions

The heart has reasons the mind knows nothing of.

—Blaise Pascal

A t a fundamental level, our minds and hearts collect our experiences and try desperately to form them into coherent patterns. Philosophers look for the logic in the theories they study. In the same way, the story of our hearts looks for ways to make sense of our experiences and personal connections. And our deepest perceptions form their own logic. We recognize this logic as statements or questions which address the most foundational meanings about the world, others, ourselves, and God. These aren't eloquent, articulated sentences but raw concepts that are the foundation of everything we believe, think, say and do. The most primitive meanings written on our hearts are called Heart Logic.

The First Sentences

From the time my (Charity's) son was born (almost three years ago at this writing), he's been making sense of the world around him. The world is full of wonders when you're new to it. I can see curiosity on his face and hear it in his voice. He wants to know who people are, when he's going to eat, and why he can't do everything he wants to do. Even in his earliest months, he began absorbing language and attaching meaning to objects. He'd put everything he could reach in his mouth—things that belonged there and plenty of things that didn't! It was his way of testing the world, making sense of shapes and textures. He's even learned that he has a voice—and he practices every pitch he can make, just for the fun of it! He has been incredibly busy making sense of the world, so no wonder he has to sleep so much!

Beyond learning that my name is Mom, there are far more important meanings. He's asking himself some important questions, even though he doesn't know he's asking them. Even before he's got the language and cognitive capacity to understand them, he's already asking questions like, "Am I loved?" "Am I safe?" "Do I trust these people?" and "Will they take care of me?" The most fundamental part of his soul wants to know if he's secure.

It doesn't take advanced language skills to ask these questions, and it doesn't take a mature perspective to intuit them. His little heart just watches, listens, assesses, and decides. As a parent, I feel a burden to get it right and make sure he doesn't doubt he's secure with me. I pray that by consistency in my love, he's realizing the world is safe and that he's infinitely valuable.

Your heart also went through the same process of watching and waiting for the first inklings of understanding. We don't usually articulate the Heart Logic questions. My young son doesn't know that he's watching for signs to measure goodness all around him, but he is. And so are you.

Even if you consider yourself to be a feeler rather than a thinker, don't dismiss the importance of Heart Logic. All of us have this primitive part that makes meaning from intuition.

Heart Logic is established very early in life. It can be revised, but your initial conclusions are often written deep in your heart, making them hard to rewrite.

All people ask these four Heart Logic questions:

1) God: Is God good? Is He really good all the time?

2) Yourself: Am I good even though I'm flawed? Am I truly valued and worthy of love?

3) Other people: Are other people good? Is there goodness among the brokenness in humanity?

4) The world: Is life good? Is life good even in the most difficult times?

Essentially, your heart wants to know if goodness exists. It wants to know if you're secure enough to trust. And it wants to know if it's secure enough to have hope. If your heart takes a deep breath and rests in trust and hope, its confidence becomes the fuel of faith. The cumulative effect? The degree to which you can understand goodness in the midst of darkness and pain determines your capacity for emotional and spiritual wellness. We'll cover this progression in detail later in this chapter.

Flawed Heart Logic

As you've observed life around you and interpreted meaning, the pen in your hand either underlined the words God wrote in His original story, affirming the security He intended you to have, or it rewrote the story, diminishing trust, limiting hope, and keeping love at arm's length.

In God's story of our lives, the answer to each of the Heart Logic questions is a resounding "yes!" But because the answers to the questions come from your heart rather than your head, they easily drown out God's truth and His promises. Even if your knowledge tells you that there's goodness around you and within you, the conclusion your heart has drawn may be that people can't be trusted, God doesn't care, and life never works out. Your heart doesn't intuit according to reason or faith. Instead, Heart Logic is absorbed by experience—and remember from Chapter 2, experience isn't always a reliable teacher.

Couples' counselor Rick Steadman comments, "The logic of the heart trumps thinking." This may sound like an oxymoron, but it's absolutely true. Many of us are very smart, and we've spent our lives living by our wits. We're pretty sure we have things figured out! But Heart Logic goes deeper—much deeper—than our thoughts. We've drawn conclusions based on our defenses and drives, not on what's really true about God, ourselves, others, and the world.

Heart Logic is influenced by what's already been written in your story. When our imperfect world has given you Sore Spots, they're often far more influential than reason and truth.

Remember that Sore Spots act as a filter to influence how you'll see the world around you. Their chief goal is to protect you from more pain, so they will try to convince you to be cautious, put up walls, or do whatever it takes to prevent more pain. Sore Spots see threats everywhere.

Insecurity and shame try to convince you that you're unworthy of love. Fear implores you to see that there's no goodness in life. Rejection tells you there's no goodness in people. Pride says, "There's no goodness in God—at least not as much as in me." The strong emotion attached to your Sore Spot makes these conclusions very convincing!

The promises God makes about truth, beauty, and goodness (Genesis 1:27, 1 Timothy 4:4, Psalm 106:1) might be stuck in your head without making the trip of the last eighteen inches into your heart.

The Silent Voice

Heart Logic is often hard to articulate because most of us have never stopped to consider these questions and discover the answers. Heart Logic derives considerable power by living in the shadowy depths beneath consciousness. As long as it remains obscure and unknown, you don't have the opportunity to evaluate it and rewrite it. You blindly follow its lead.

Even if you don't realize you've asked these crucial questions, your answers still guide your thinking and your actions and define your sense of meaning. You'll learn much more about your more conscious thinking and doing in Chapter 7. But for now, uncover the hidden layer of your heart where the most primitive meanings have been written.

The Four Heart Logic Questions

Let's take a deeper look at the four Heart Logic questions. You might already be wondering how your heart has answered them. It's easy to assume that you've adopted God's answers, especially if you're a believer and think you're supposed to know these things. But don't jump to conclusions too quickly. Challenge yourself to let your heart answer these questions, not just your head.

1) *Is God good? Is He really good all the time?*

At some point, you've decided whether or not God is good. You've decided whether He has your best interests in mind and whether He's on your side. You've decided whether He's good even if things get hard and He doesn't take away the struggles. You've decided if He's worthy of your giving the most valuable part of you—your trust.

In the original story God wrote for our hearts, the sentence "God is good all the time" is written deep within. John reminds us, "Whoever does not love does not know God, because God is love" (1 John 4:8). There's no exception, no end, and no condition to God's goodness. He is supremely good and worthy of trust.

God was still good when He let Job suffer by his livestock being stolen, his servants killed, and even his sons and daughters murdered (Job 1:12-19). God was good when He cursed the Egyptians and let them be struck down (Ezekiel 32:15). God is good even when it feels like you're being crushed by an unbearable weight that won't let up.

Flawed, pain-filled Heart Shapers don't mirror God's unrelenting goodness, and it confuses us.

The imperfect influences of life have kept your eyes focused on the pain of the past rather than the reality of God's goodness—especially in times of suffering. The brokenness around you may have convinced you that a God who loves you wouldn't allow these things to happen to you. Even the most faithful among us can wrestle with one of the world's most difficult questions: "Why do bad things happen to good people?"

A mom who's loved Jesus her whole life can have a hard time believing He's on her side when her five-year-old child gets leukemia. A man who has given his life to Christ but whose family has suffered repeated disease and death can believe God loves everyone else but not him. And a Christian leader who has felt God's blessing assumes there are exceptions to God's goodness when he is unexpectedly fired.

Gerald May describes the struggle to grow in his faith: "I know that God is loving and that God's loving is trustworthy. I know this directly, through the experience of my life. There have been plenty of times of doubt, especially when I used to believe that trusting God's goodness meant I would not be hurt. But having been hurt quite a bit, I know God's goodness goes deeper than all pleasure and pain; it embraces them both."[4]

When devastating things happen that push the limits of our logic, our humanity cries, "If I can just understand this, I can believe." But faith says, "When I can't understand it, can't fix it, and can't control it, I'll still trust." Trust protects us from the pit of despair we fall into when our inability to understand makes us conclude God isn't wise, good, or reliable.

Maybe the people who were supposed to love you have failed to love you well. Maybe people close to you have put conditions on their love. Or maybe you couldn't trust that they were always going to be there for you. Their example makes it easy to believe the day is coming (or has already arrived) when God will stop loving you. But God's love never fails.

Your heart may think that God's justice requires Him to remove His love because of your sin. But God's goodness and justice coexist. With God's new covenant, He has turned His wrath away from the believer and reserved it only for those who reject Him. Isaiah shares God's promise of salvation: "'This exile is just like the days of Noah for me: I promised then that the waters of Noah would never again flood the earth. I'm promising now no more anger, no more dressing

---

4   Cited by Brennan Manning in *Ruthless Trust* (New York: HarperOne, 2000), p. 22.

you down. For even if the mountains walk away and the hills fall to pieces, My love won't walk away from you, my covenant commitment of peace won't fall apart.' The God who has compassion on you says so" (Isaiah 54:9-10, MSG). Believers are secure with God, even in our imperfections, because God's grace is greater than all our sins. God doesn't withdraw His affection or limit His mercy when those who have chosen to believe in Him sin.

Your answer to the question, "Is God good all the time?" carries important implications for your ability to fare well in this difficult world. When you don't believe you've been good enough to earn God's love, you can rest in knowing that even when you fall short, God calls you "loved, forgiven, and accepted" because of His goodness and grace. When other people fail you, you find solace in God still being on your side. And when the world is unkind, you remember that God is still the benevolent authority over it all. If you don't believe God is good all the time, you might feel overwhelmed by the difficulties of life. You might feel helpless, hopeless, angry, or defeated, with nothing to stand on.

Has this sentence really been written on your heart, "God is good all the time"?

Perhaps you've been convinced enough to trust that God is good with only rare exceptions. Maybe you've seen enough goodness to believe that He's good to other people, just not always to you, so you aren't fully sold on the idea that He's good *all the time*.

God wants you to know His goodness in the depths of your soul. Moving this truth into your heart's story is an irreplaceable resource in living well when we encounter heartaches and setbacks.

2) *Yourself: Am I good even though I'm flawed? Am I truly valued*
   and worthy of love?

Your heart has wondered, "Am I valued? Am I truly worthy of
love?" You wanted to know if you measure up and are accepted by
God. Maybe you've wondered if you measure up to people too. You've
asked yourself whether you are wanted. You've tried hard to present
yourself to God and others as a decent and competent person...but is
that enough?

Maybe you've also wondered, "Is there still goodness in me even
though I'm such a screw-up sometimes? Are God's grace and mercy
enough to overcome my dark moments?" Or perhaps you've asked,
"Is it remotely possible that my goodness isn't solely determined by
my performance? Can I really live in the freedom of having nothing
to prove?"

In the bigger, better, greater story that God wrote for your heart,
the sentences, "I'm good even though I'm flawed. I'm valuable, and
I'm worthy of love," are written deep within.

God says that all of His creation is good (Genesis 1:31), but He
goes beyond that: He calls you by name and declares that you are good
(Isaiah 43:1). He doesn't just put up with you—He delights in you!
(Romans 8:39, Zephaniah 3:17) *Delight* is a powerful word. It means
He cherishes you. And it's not because of your perfection or accom-
plishments, but because you belong to Him. He calls you His own
even in your weakness and even in your sin because His grace and
mercy are sufficient (2 Corinthians 12:9). He says that your worth isn't
dependent on others seeing it (Luke 12:6-7). That's right—even when
someone else fails to see your value, you're of infinite value to God,

worth more to Him than all the stars in the sky and all the jewels in the earth!

But the problem is that life doesn't always communicate that you're good, wanted, or worthy. Faulty Heart Logic says things like, "I'm not enough," "I'm only as good as my last performance," and "I'm a failure."

Once I (Charity) asked a woman to describe a picture that showed her relationship with God. She described a scene with Jesus in the middle of a crowd loving on everyone. He was engaged with the people, smiling at them, and putting His arms around them. She was animated and excited as she described the good God she saw.

Then I asked her, "Where are you in the picture?" She dropped her eyes to the floor and said, "I'm behind the crowd looking on." That was a powerful statement. She believed wholeheartedly that God loves people, but somehow she had made herself the exception.

You may believe that you're also an exception to God's love. You may believe He loves His creation, and you mean it when you share with others how much God loves them. But do you secretly picture God with a look of disappointment on His face when He looks at you? Is your heart convinced that others are capable of pleasing God but you just can't?

Maybe you've had a parent that was never quite pleased, no matter how well you did, and you assume that God is just like your parent. Maybe you were the forgotten one growing up, and you feel like God has forgotten you, too. Maybe you've been rejected, and the cloud of rejection has overshadowed God's declaration of your value. Perhaps you're convinced that you've abused God's grace one too many times, and your self-inflicted shame has turned God's smile into a scowl. Perhaps you can't get your critical mom's voice out of your head, the voice that keeps telling you that you didn't do it quite right, so you can't receive God's freely given love. In the depths of our hearts, those Heart Shapers can negate the power of God's unshakable stamp of approval.

Our goodness is bestowed on us by God as we believe in Him. Maybe you believe in your inherent goodness as a creation of Christ, but you have yet to overcome all the extra rules and obligations you've created to determine your worth, like perfect performance or earning approval. Perhaps you wrestle with perfectionistic standards. You have to learn to rest in God's delight when others don't delight in you. Or you need to forgive yourself for things God has long ago forgiven you for. You aren't the exception to God's love and approval!

You are called to live in freedom from proving yourself so that your performance can be about your service and not yourself.

So, is this written on your heart: "I'm good even though I'm flawed. I'm valuable and I'm worthy of love"?

3) *Are other people good? Is there goodness among the brokenness in humanity?*

Your heart has used its "sixth sense" to determine if people around you are good and trustworthy. We generally extrapolate our perceptions: When we're young, if someone has hurt us badly, we often assume others will hurt us, so we erect defenses. But if we grew up in a stable, loving environment, we will probably gain the ability to see that all of us are, to some degree, shades of gray. Your heart has already come to crucial answers to the questions: "Should I trust people?" "Who should I trust, and who earns at least some skepticism?" "Are relationships worth it?" "Can I tolerate others' imperfections?" "Can goodness and brokenness coexist in the same person?" And, "Do all people have at least a measure of good—the image of God—in them?"

God's story includes the phrase, "There is goodness in humanity, even though there's brokenness in it."

Each one of us bears God's image (Genesis 1:26-27), but our brokenness is very real. The image of God is tarnished in all of us, and in some, it's barely recognizable. No one is untouched by the fall; a sinful nature is in the bones of humanity. That leads people to do some really damaging, hurtful things (Matthew 5:19; Matthew 7:15) that display their brokenness and damage your heart.

All relationships come with risks of pain, rejection, and wounding. Maybe you've had an absent parent, or you've been abused. Perhaps your spouse has cheated on you. Maybe you've been lied to again and again. Maybe your spouse isn't attentive. After the hurt, faulty Heart Logic shouts that all people are rotten to the core!

Hurt tells you to put your guard up, notice the bad in others and ignore the good. You might overgeneralize, seeing everyone as a potential threat, a conclusion that makes you cynical. Your heart reminds you that people have power to hurt you, and it will tell you that you shouldn't trust...anyone...ever.

When we're deeply hurt, we often see the person as a two-dimensional character: a thief, a liar, an addict, an abuser. In our reaction to the pain, we can't see anything good in him or her. You're sure you'd be a fool to see goodness in the person who'd so blatantly, and maybe intentionally, hurt you. What about the parent who looked into your fearful eyes and still chose to hit you? What about the mentor who betrayed your trust and told others your secrets? Can there be good even in those who have abused power, acted cold-heartedly, and taken pleasure in your pain?

Using the book of Proverbs, psychologist Henry Cloud describes three types of people: wise, foolish, and evil.[5] Dr. Cloud explains how these types of people receive feedback and how to relate to them. We want to use his concepts and ask, "Does goodness exist in all three?"

Wise people are known for being good and kind. They have developed a beautiful blend of humility and boldness. A few characteristics from Proverbs are used to describe the wise: "uses his tongue to bring healing" (12:18), "brings joy to his parents" (10:1), and "keeps himself under control" (29:11) But wise people are affected by the fall and have some darkness in them. They're broken, but they lean hard into God's goodness and grace. We might say that wise people are very good at repentance. They are filled with "living water" that overflows into the lives of others.

Foolish people display far more brokenness. Proverbs says plenty about the fool: "A fool's mouth is his ruin, and his lips are a snare to his soul" (18:7), "doing wrong is fun for him" (10:23), and "their mouths pour out folly" (15:2). But even people who ruin their own lives and others have hints of the image of God. Their brokenness gets the best of them far too often, but some good exists in them, even if it's dormant.

---

5 "Wise, Foolish, or Evil: Which One Are You Going to Be?" Henry Cloud, Global Leadership, June 1, 2017, https://globalleadership.org/articles/leading-others/wise-foolish-evil-one-going-dr-henry-cloud/

We see that good and brokenness coexist, and the presence of brokenness doesn't exclude goodness. In our experience, there's a lot of room for goodness to grow, even in the fools who do stupid, self-destructive things. They desperately need to follow the pathway of redemption and trust God to rewrite their stories!

But some people are genuinely evil people. Proverbs describes the evil as "far from the Lord" (15:29). It says their "perverted hearts plot evil" (6:14) and they "constantly stir up trouble" (6:14). Evil people are adamantly opposed to God. They abuse without remorse, use cruelty to dominate, and lie with a straight face. Do certain faces come to mind when you read this description? It's easy to conclude that these people have totally black hearts—no love, no light, no truth. The image of God is much harder to see in them.

Even though good is compromised in the foolish and is seemingly absent in those who are evil, should we see all of humanity as bad? Does it mean that our starting place should be mistrust?

We need to be careful about using extreme labels like "evil." It's easy to vilify people who have hurt you. Of the people who have hurt you, someone may be genuinely evil, but probably far more are foolish. You might label some as evil who are just foolish because you want revenge or want to self-protect, and the label is a way to write them off as unredeemable. We shouldn't excuse their behavior, and we must be honest about the wounds, but sometimes people are following the example set by their role models. They're wounded, too, and "hurt people hurt people." Brokenness isn't the same as evil.

All of us have wounds, and all of us have choices about trust and mistrust. Unhealthy Heart Logic concludes that people aren't trustworthy. And if you start from a place of mistrust, believing people are bad until they prove otherwise, you will have little capacity to trust when someone proves to be honorable and honest.

Healthy Heart Logic enables you to trust wisely. If you start from a position of trust, believing people are good until they prove otherwise, you're able to choose whom you trust, how much you trust, and how to repair broken trust.

So, will you begin from a position of trust or mistrust?

Is this sentence written deep in your heart: "Is there goodness among the brokenness in humanity?"

4) *Is life good? Is life good even in the most difficult times?*

Actress Katharine Hepburn remarked, "Life is hard. After all, it kills you."[6] As you grew up, your heart drew conclusions about life in general, not just particular people. It learned to interpret situations, especially difficult ones, as cataclysmic or bumps in the road. It formed assumptions that everything and everyone is a threat, or that God can bring good out of the most tragic circumstances.

God injects good into our lives. Jesus explained, "When Jesus spoke again to the people, he said, 'I am the light of the world. Whoever follows me will never walk in darkness but will have the light of life'" (John 8:12). But life doesn't always feel very good. In fact, it seems downright pointless at times. Suffering is part of human experience, and for some of us, it feels like the dominant narrative.

Everything about life felt hard to Maryann. Her life started with challenge, which set the stage for her. She was born 12 weeks early and

---

6   Katharine Hepburn, *Me: Stories of My Life* (New York: Knopf, 1991), p. 219.

had some complications that followed her into childhood, leaving her chronically sick. She wrestled with digestive issues and an autoimmune disease for most of her life. She spent many days on the couch with no energy. Her marriage felt hard too. Her friend described her husband as a bully, and she was right. He was condescending and had no interest in hearing how his attitude affected Maryann's heart. She believed she was losing both battles: with her body and with her husband. Maryann didn't see much goodness in life; it just felt hard—very hard. Hope had vanished; her eyes were fixed on her pain.

Imperfect Heart Logic says that life is just hard, there's no purpose in suffering, and there's no hope when things get tough. When our hearts consider these statements to be irrefutable facts, we become defeated and overwhelmed.

But God says that life is good despite the pain. He never promised it would be easy, but in the midst of the trouble, we can take heart because He has overcome the world (John 16:33). God offers us an eternal promise (John 3:16) beyond the trouble we face, and this promise gives us hope in the middle of our struggles: It won't always be this hard. Hope brings light into our darkness, and it shines most brightly in the presence of God. In his most famous psalm, David reminds us: "Even though I walk through the darkest valley, I will fear no evil, for you are with me; your rod and your staff, they comfort me" (Psalm 23:4).

God provides purpose in the midst of pain. As we've seen, Paul explained that "suffering produces perseverance; perseverance, character; and character, hope" (Romans 5:3-4). And he told the Philippians that suffering is a part of life: "There's far more to this life than trusting in Christ. There's also suffering for him. And the suffering is as much a gift as the trusting" (Philippians 1:29, MSG). It's not a gift we asked for, but God is up to something. He's shaping character in you (James 1:2-4, Romans 5:2b-5), He's equipping you to minister to others (2 Corinthians 1:3-4), and He's has a thousand purposes intricately woven into the ripple effects of an event. Whether it was God's original plan for the suffering to happen, or He is just capitalizing on the opportunity, God will step in to create purpose in our pain (Romans 8:28). The growth that happens in hardship transforms some of the darkness into light, hope, and love.

Life most certainly *is* hard. And for some, it's excruciating.

Nevertheless, is this sentence written upon your heart, "Life is good, even though it can be really hard"?

The Implications of Your Answers

If you answer "no" to any of the Heart Logic questions, it sets you up for a host of problems that can culminate in hopelessness and helplessness. If you aren't convinced life is good, you might hide from any risks or threats, try desperately (to no avail) to control it, or settle for an empty life and be robbed of contentment. If you don't believe you have any good in you, you might live with a cloud of shame or the burden of perfectionism (or both). If you don't believe others have any good in them, you might keep your guard up or exhaust yourself trying to stay one step ahead to remain in control. If you don't believe God is good, you might rely on yourself and miss all the resources He provides. All of these conclusions create gaps in your life.

Sore Spots are inextricably linked to faulty Heart Logic Questions: Our pain causes us to give the wrong answers to the questions. But the healing of Sore Spots paves the way to draw very different conclusions—positive ones—to the questions.

Each "yes" you give to a Heart Logic question helps you develop critical factors that become your pathway across your gap: security, trust, hope, and faith.

It begins by building a bedrock of security through saying "yes" to the Heart Logic questions. Think about it.

When your heart asks, "Is God good?" it's wondering if you're safe and secure with Him.

When your heart asks, "Am I good?" it's wondering if you can be secure in who you are.

When your heart asks, "Are other people good?" it's wondering whether it's safe to trust them.

When your heart asks, "Is life good?" it's wondering if God has a purpose even in the most difficult times.

For Christians, security comes from an unexpected source. Pastor and author Tim Keller comments, "The more you see your own flaws and sins the more precious, electrifying, and amazing God's grace appears to you."[7] In the world, we look for security by impressing people and accomplishing great things, but with God, security comes from the profound understanding that He knows the worst about us and loves us still. Security is also found as we affirm the true character of God, which gives us the ability to courageously release control when we can't understand. Security grows when we see enough good

---

7   Tim Keller, *Gospel in Life Study Guide: Grace Changes Everything* (Grand Rapids: Zondervan, 2010), p. 29.

in humanity to begin to believe the best in someone. Security is found too in the profound ability to see beyond the pain when our worst nightmares happen, but we still lean into the comfort of Jesus.

With a foundation of security, you develop a capacity for trust and hope. And trust and hope become the planks of the bridge across your gap by leading you into deeper faith.

Will You Trust?

You can go to church your whole life, authentically love God, and yet have a seed of mistrust at the shadowy level of Heart Logic. Something in you doubts His unwavering goodness. You may have capacity for trust in some ways, like trusting you'll be with Him in heaven, but you may not be able (or willing) to trust Him with your daily decisions. Or perhaps you can trust Him to take care of others but not when the matter gets a little more personal.

You have to be convinced it's safe to trust God fully and without condition by believing in His unwavering goodness. You need the security to let go of what makes sense to you, turn your palms up, and prayerfully say, "Your will be done."

You also need to conclude there's at least some goodness in others even though they're terribly flawed. Will you trust people enough to journey with them through life? Will you let them in far enough to genuinely know you so they can bring out the best in you? And do you have the wisdom and strength to avoid trusting those who have proven they aren't trustworthy?

If your Heart Logic tells you it's not safe to trust anyone, you'll keep your guard up and have surface-level relationships at best. You'll hide your true thoughts and feelings. You'll rely too much on yourself. You'll listen to your own voice too much and often feel alone. Have you ever noticed that your mistrust of others brings out the worst in them while trusting them tends to bring out the best?

Trust is a nonnegotiable ingredient in healthy relationships. Healthy people capable of healthy relationships are positioned with a reservoir of trust to share with others—that's part of the genius God gives us. With the capacity for trust, you're able to live vulnerably, collaborate, and have effective teamwork. But trusting others requires that you believe in the goodness of humanity to some degree so that you can see when people are trustworthy.

We saw earlier that it's essential to begin from a place of trust. When we have the capacity to trust wisely, we can move toward people and offer authentic connections, and back away when necessary.

The third area is trusting in your capacity for goodness. We don't mean being full of self-sufficiency but full of self-esteem. Trusting your goodness means being fully convinced that you are who God says you are so that you show up and use your God-given voice. Will you trust in yourself enough to embrace who God made you to be? Will you trust that you are infinitely valuable because of God's grace, even though you're flawed and broken?

Remember, security isn't built on your own greatness. It rests in God's grace, which covers your inadequacies and blemishes. You trust the Holy Spirit's presence in you, which makes you wiser and stronger. When you trust the esteem that God bestows upon you it frees you from self-absorption and puts your attention more and more on your service instead of self.

When your Heart Logic doesn't trust in your value, self-doubt clouds your thoughts. It muzzles your voice, paralyzes you from God-directed action, and makes you second-guess yourself. But trusting who you are allows you to live to the full capacity in the story God edits for you. It allows you to live with holy boldness and follow God's will without unnecessary limitations.

The fourth area is trusting that life is good no matter how hard so that you can find resilience when you need it most. Will believing in God's purpose in pain give you the fuel you need to get back up after life has pummeled you once again? Will a warrior spirit rise up in you because your heart is tethered so tightly to God's promises of love, purpose, and provision that outweigh and overshadow any hardship?

Has your heart decided that it's safe to trust?

Will You Have Hope?

Saying "yes" to the Heart Logic Questions also renews our hope.

Hope expects God to reveal His goodness and believes He has a good purpose even when we don't see it. Hope in God gives you the ability to believe in something greater than the pain of the present, knowing that He has the power to redeem any situation and turn darkness to light.

When your Heart Logic tells you there's nothing to hope in, you give up. You resign yourself to mediocrity—or worse. You expect the worst and lose the capacity for joy. Without hope, you get swallowed up by problems and hear nothing but the cries of agony from your heart. Hope in your value is believing you're capable of rising beyond what you are now.

Hope in the goodness of others gives you the ability to see into their hearts to find goodness as well as their brokenness. It allows you to expect to encounter good in people.

Hope gives you the capacity to live well in a difficult world. It's your leg to stand on when you feel you can't go on. Hope is what motivates you to keep going when logic tells you it's hopeless. Hope is water for a soul wandering in the desert.

And hope, in spite of the heartaches and difficulties, is believing in the promise of eternal life, which takes away the power of despair.

Has your heart decided it's safe to have hope?

Trust + Hope = Faith

As you build deeply rooted trust and hope by finding positive answers to the Heart Logic questions, you're building your capacity for a bigger, more robust faith.

Martin Luther said, "Faith is a living, bold trust in God's grace, so certain of God's favor that it would risk death a thousand times trusting in it. Such confidence and knowledge of God's grace makes you happy, joyful and bold in your relationship to God and all creatures."[8] To have "bold trust" we need "confidence and knowledge of God's grace." We can be "so certain of God's favor that we would risk death a thousand times."

---

8   Martin Luther's Definition of Faith: An excerpt from "An Introduction to St. Paul's Letter to the Romans," Luther's German Bible of 1522 by Martin Luther, 1483-1546. Translated by Rev. Robert E. Smith from DR. MARTIN LUTHER'S VERMISCHTE DEUTSCHE SCHRIFTEN. Johann K. Irmischer, ed. Vol. 63(Erlangen: Heyder and Zimmer, 1854), pp.124-125. [EA 63:124-125] August 1994.

The writer to the Hebrews affirms Luther's conviction: "Faith is the assurance of things you have hoped for, the absolute conviction that there are realities you've never seen" (Hebrews 11:1, Voice).

Aligning all of your Heart Logic's conclusions with God's perspective produces deep-rooted trust and uncrushable hope, and ultimately, deeper faith than you've ever known!

Faith is the essence of the Christian walk. Positive answers to the Heart Logic questions form the cornerstone of a strong relationship with Christ. There's no working around imperfectly written Heart Logic. There's no way to get authentic, sold-out faith without the hope and trust that come from being convinced of God's goodness, of your goodness (because of Him), in people, and in life.

These are essential steps toward wholehearted living, of a rewritten story that's unhindered by fear, insecurity, and bondage. Sometimes, new believers are more open to the process of change than those who have been Christians for many years. The "seasoned" believers have a harder time admitting their concept of God hasn't been as accurate as they thought. It takes enormous courage for anyone to open up to the long-buried wounds, resentments, and shame, but in our experience, Christian leaders often are the most resistant. But when they do, a lifetime of Bible study finds new meaning, concepts of God's grace are farther reaching, and their leadership becomes infused with faith, hope, and love.

Reflection

What conclusions have been written on your heart to these questions:

- *Is God good? Is He really good all the time?*

- *Am I good even though I'm flawed? Am I valued, and am I truly worthy of love?*

- *Are people good? Is there goodness, even among the brokenness in humanity?*

- *Is life good? Is life good even in the most difficult times?*

How have your answers to the Heart Logic questions impacted your ability to trust?

How have your answers impacted your ability to have hope?

Understanding Heart Logic may seem like it's all up to you, but what role does God play in revealing it and giving you wisdom about how to address it?

CHAPTER 6

Heart Logic: Correcting Flawed Assumptions

Character is both developed and revealed by tests, and all of life is a test.

—RICK WARREN

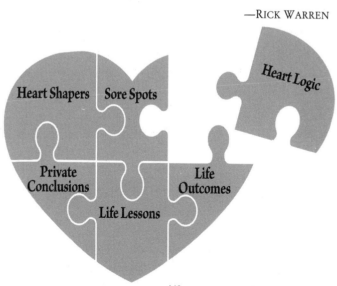

I n the last chapter, we identified common answers to the four Heart Logic questions. Of course, people may answer some affirmatively and others negatively. Based on the Heart Shapers you've encountered, your heart might answer "yes" to some and "no" to others. Your answers interact to shape your trajectory toward (or away from) hope and trust. The implications are far-reaching when you aren't able to say "yes" to all four.

As we've seen, the human heart wants to avoid pain at all costs. One of the ways Christians avoid it is by giving quick, affirmative answers to the Heart Logic Questions. We might say, "Oh, yes, God is good!" But it's what we've always said, and the statement isn't born out in our level of trust and love for God. Or we might say, "I'm good," to hide our shame. We might say, "Yes, people are good," because admitting someone is unkind and untrustworthy would force us to have some hard conversations. And we easily pronounce, "Life is good," though we're on the edge of burnout and full of anxiety. The "yeses" we give to the Heart Logic Questions can't be superficial or rote; they must be genuine. Fear keeps us from honesty, but we have a God who knows the worst about us and loves us still. We can trust Him.

Consider these three examples of people who wrestled with their answers to the questions:

1) *If God isn't good and life isn't good, then life isn't worth living.*

Noelle was convinced that God made a mistake when He allowed her to be born. She saw no purpose for living a life that kept beating her up. She had suffered from physical abuse by her father and emotional distance from her mother, and when she grew up, she didn't have the ability to choose wisely in a spouse. Her emotionally abusive husband, coupled with nagging pain from earlier abuse and chronic financial struggles, demoralized her. Noelle was tired of trying to put the pieces back together from one calamity just to have her world shaken by the next one.

Noelle knew other people had hard lives. She heard some of them quote Romans 8:28: "And we know that in all things God works for the good of those who love him, who have been called according to his purpose." Somehow, the verse seemed to comfort them, but she found no peace in it.

The deepest levels of Noelle's heart didn't believe that God was for her. On some level, she believed He loved her, but apparently He didn't love her enough to answer her prayers to stop the chaos and pain. Her hopelessness crushed her spirit. She didn't see any point in living if God couldn't be trusted.

Noelle's predicament is like that of many others. If life is hard and you don't believe God is good, you won't be able to trust Him and experience wisdom and peace when hardships happen. You'll conclude that life just isn't worth it. You'll have no resiliency to carry you through hard times. Only those who can say, "This is hard, but I know my good God is in it with me," can have God's perspective about the pain and come out the victor. We need a deep reservoir of faith in God's benevolent sovereignty to navigate life in a difficult world. Faith becomes our resource to find purpose and hope in hard times.

The prophet Isaiah assures us, "So do not fear, for I am with you; do not be dismayed, for I am your God. I will strengthen you and help you; I will uphold you with my righteous right hand" (Isaiah 41:10).

2) *If people are good but God isn't, I need to trust them instead of God.*

If you're convinced that people have some intrinsic goodness in them, your starting place will be to trust them, which is healthy. You'll be willing to befriend someone who feels alone. You'll have compassion for those who have royally messed up their lives. But if you blindly trust people because you don't trust God, you'll be in trouble. If you're not convinced of God's goodness, you'll look to other people for your security, your worth, your belonging, and your identity—and they cannot be your primary source for these essentials. Out of your need to lean on someone, you may become overly dependent on people.

Life taught Martin that God wasn't trustworthy. Years ago, he prayed over some business decisions and thought he was following God's lead, but they became major losses. He'd also been through the loss of three pregnancies with his wife and couldn't understand why God wouldn't give them the child they wanted. To Martin, God certainly didn't feel present and trustworthy.

As the heartaches multiplied, Martin listened more to people and less to God. When he had decisions to make, he picked up the phone and called his friends for advice—he rarely prayed. When he needed to feel a sense of value, he did something that was sure to win a compliment from his boss or his wife instead of soaking up God's abundant love. Over time, the faith and reliance Martin once had in God was eroded, and he looked to people to give him acceptance and meaning.

We need to be wise in our trust of people, but we need to have ultimate trust in God. People have some goodness in them, but they're flawed. God is good, righteous, faithful, kind, and just. "In him there is no darkness at all" (1 John 1:5).

3) *If life isn't good (or at least isn't very good), then God can't be good.*

How many times have you been frustrated with God for letting hard things happen to you? Have you had difficulty reconciling your pain with the goodness of God? If you have, you're in good company.

When life is falling apart, when you just can't catch a break, or when unjust things keep happening, it's easy for a piece of your heart to wonder if God is good after all. Maybe you've been through far too much disappointment, and you can't take any more. Your pain is telling you that God doesn't really care.

As Sherry shared her story with me, she compared her ongoing suffering to feeling like a battered wife who keeps coming back for more. She talked about how her discomfort was tolerable for a while because she kept digging deeper into God's love. But then, she reached her limit. At that point she was sure she'd learned whatever lesson God was teaching her. When she could no longer see any purpose in the unrelenting pain, God appeared to be reckless and heartless. She wondered if God was punishing her. She just didn't feel like He had compassion for her in her struggle. The disappointment she felt from unanswered prayers eventually gave her a new expectation: She was sure that no matter how much she prayed, God would ignore her. But out of a sense of duty—not hope—she didn't stop praying. That's why she felt like a battered wife who kept returning for another beating.

When suffering starts, you might drop to your knees in desperate prayer. But when it feels like nothing is happening, you start asking, "Where are you God? Do you even notice? Do you really care?"

Maybe you've never had anyone protect you, defend you, or really care for you, and you've been desperate for a God who would. But now it seems that He's like all the rest. You draw the painful conclusion that God can't be good if He lets you be pulled under the waves.

The capacity life has for goodness doesn't mirror God's capacity for goodness. God is good even on the worst day of your life. God is good because He is present in your pain (Psalm 34:18). He may rescue you out of your pain, but more often, He walks with you in the middle of it. In the process, He gives you more insight, more compassion, and more strength. God is good even when your suffering doesn't stop. We look again to Isaiah for wisdom: "Even though the Lord has fed you the bitter food of adversity and offered you the water of oppression, your great Teacher will reveal Himself to you; your eyes will see Him" (Isaiah 30:20, Voice). As crazy as it sounds, giving us adversity is part of God's goodness because He uses it to accomplish His good (if sometimes inscrutable) purposes. As we learn to trust God in difficult times, we develop stronger faith muscles, our compassion for others deepens, and we experience God's love and strength at a far deeper level. We no longer demand to be in control because we're assured that God, our sovereign King, holds all things in His hands.

Perhaps you've been taught that if you're faithful enough, God will protect you from harm. That promise sounds good, but only to those who aren't suffering! If we believe this wrong interpretation of Scripture, we become confused when hardships happen, then we're full of self-pity, and then we're furious that God didn't come through "like He promised." As we gain more insight and see that this promise is a lie, we become angry at the teachers who misled us and doubled the pain we experienced.

Too many Christians believe that God can't be good unless their lives are always good. And others have been in spiritual battle so long that they feel abandoned by God. If this is your understanding, your image of God needs some adjustment, so you can see God as both good *and* inscrutable. He always knows what He's doing, but we only see a small fraction of His plans.

Three Phases of Heart Logic

We can identify three major phases in our development of Heart Logic. The first phase establishes it. We begin answering the Heart Logic questions before we even learn how to talk and walk. But our answers usually don't stand unchallenged very long. Many of us find ourselves wrestling with the conclusions our hearts have drawn when something happens that opposes them.

The second and third phases provide opportunities to resolve and redeem imperfect Heart Logic. The resolution of flawed Heart

Logic may not be an intentional process; it may be a natural part of emotional and spiritual growth. Let's examine the three phases.

1) *Childhood*

Heart Logic is established very early in life. As a young child, you answered the questions by intuiting the world around you, rather than logically forming your perceptions. You watched your parents, other caregivers, and siblings, and you drew implications about God, yourself, others, and the world. Experience, rather than God and His Word, was your teacher.

Your family of origin is the crucible of early development. You instinctively asked yourself questions like, "Does my family love me?" "Can I trust my parents (or other caregivers)?" "Do I feel safe and cared for in my family?" Your answers to these questions went a long way to shape who you are and what you believe. While your answers can be reshaped over time, a strong foundation was set quite early.

2) *When you choose to follow Christ*

A golden opportunity for challenging flawed Heart Logic happens at the time you accept Christ. Some decisions you make in the process of accepting Christ naturally challenge faulty Heart Logic. In considering the gospel of grace, you're faced with the question, "Is God good?" You must realize that, in fact, He's good (at least to some degree) in order to want to follow Him. You believe that He brings healing and purpose into the brokenness of the world. That's exactly what you trust He'll do in your broken world! Of course, none of us fully comprehends the nature of God, and at the beginning of one's faith journey, some of us are reserved in our trust in who God is and what He'll do. It's a "wait and see" mentality: "I'll choose to believe, but let's really see how this life with God goes before I give away ALL of my trust."

Accepting Christ also gives opportunities to come face-to-face with other truths that are different from your life experience. As you get to know God's ways and Word, you may learn for the first time that your worth isn't based on your performance, and this truth helps you realize that God loves us in spite of our performances, not because of them. The experience of grace you encounter at the cross gives you new eyes to see other people and love them the way God loves you. You might learn about God's presence in the midst of hard circumstances and find God to be "a very present help in times of trouble" (Psalm 46:1).

As you learn these truths, you might connect the dots in Scripture and reason your way to trust and hope. Or it might be more of an emotional experience that gets you there. You might feel God's powerful presence or see Him work in a mighty way, and the wonder of His love may instill hope and trust in you. No matter your method of arrival, your new faith in Christ may go a long way to shape affirmative answers to the Heart Logic questions.

However, if the moment of accepting Christ were all it took to rewrite flawed heart logic, we'd only see seasoned Christians with full security in who they are never holding back in their trust in God. For many of us, the flawed story of our hearts just won't let go yet, and it takes the process of growing and maturing in Christ to let God fully rewrite our Heart Logic.

3) *As you grow and mature in Christ*

The third opportunity to revise your Heart Logic happens as you grow in your relationship with Jesus.

Some accepted Christ before they had the cognitive and emotional capacity to evaluate their Heart Logic—or maybe it was still forming. Perhaps that left many unaware of the incongruences between their Heart Logic and the truth of God, or they were unaware of the collisions between their false assumptions and God's truth.

As a growing disciple, you experience deeper levels of understanding about God's Word and ways, and the process of maturing gives you a new set of lenses to evaluate people and situations. You let wise believers speak into your life, giving them the opportunity to challenge your Heart Logic, and you become more open to hearing the voice of the Holy Spirit whispering His truths. Along the way, you have many corrective experiences that rewrite imperfect Heart Logic into healthy Heart Logic.

However, as we grow, we're not immune to setbacks. Pain, heartache, loss, trauma, injustice, and the unexpected can cause us to take steps backward. Even if we've been sold-out in our faith, hard moments can create nagging doubts.

At the time you trusted Christ as your Savior, you may not have had to walk through pain that tested your heart's conclusions. It's much easier for Heart Logic to match up with God's perspective when you're five years old and life hasn't been all that hard yet! But what about when you're 55, and you've lived decades with pain, loss, and heartaches? Maybe you've been deeply perplexed by unanswered prayers, a child won't talk to you, your marriage has grown cold, or a critical boss keeps telling you that you aren't enough. You have to decide if you really believe in any goodness at all. You have countless opportunities to evaluate what your heart believes, and each time you have a choice: to answer "yes" or "no" to the Heart Logic questions.

How will you answer hard questions like, "Why do bad things happen to good people?" or "If God is all-powerful, why does He keep letting me suffer when I'm sure I've learned all I can learn from this?" As you wrestle with the answers, you'll go deeper into God's promises, and you'll find that He has purposes you never dreamed of.

At the end of my (John's) graduate studies at Indiana State University, I was subjected to what my colleagues and I called "the inquisition": the written comprehensive exam and orals in front of professors in the department. My inherent question, given my compulsion to never look stupid and to always be right, was clear: "Will I look like a fool, or will I be brilliant?" I felt the pressure so powerfully that I had a panic attack on one of the mornings of the written comps.

Two weeks after the comps, it was time for orals. I had learned my scores for the written part, but I knew the orals gave me a chance to overcome any deficiencies in what I'd written. Just before I walked into the room, my doctoral advisor, Dr. Andy Horne, pulled me aside and told me, "I'm not letting you out of the room until you say, 'I don't know,' three times." I was stunned. I'd spent my entire life making sure I never had to say, "I don't know." His advice was so far afield from my assumptions about the way life had to work that after a few seconds, it didn't even register any longer in my mind. Then he smiled and said, "Are you ready? Okay, let's go." He opened the door, and we walked in.

After about 90 minutes of answering the professors' questions, a committee member asked about a particular study. I fumbled with my answer, trying to appear knowledgeable, and cited a study that I did not know the details of. From the look on his face, it was obvious the professor didn't buy what I was saying. So, he asked me for the details of the study, and I had nothing! What I did have was a terrible sinking feeling. My career hadn't even started, and it was already over. I felt so stupid. After a couple of follow-up questions, I was in abject despair, and I told the panel, "I'm sorry, but I don't know." I believed I was exposed as a colossal fraud, but Dr. Horne smiled and said, "Let's move on."

After about 30 minutes, another professor asked me a question. This time, I decided against trying to look brilliant when I didn't have the answer. I told the professors, "I . . . I just don't know." Despair had found a new low of demoralization, but again, Dr. Horne said in the most pleasant tone, "Let's move on."

After about 10 more minutes of questions and answers, the light bulb came on. I remembered what Dr. Horne had said before we walked into the room, and I realized it wasn't a flaw—at least in his eyes—to be uninformed, as long as I was honest. One of the professors asked me a question. I knew the answer, but I looked at the panel and said, "I don't know." Dr. Horne smiled, "We're done here." And the orals were over.

This experience gave me insight I'd never had before. I had believed that the only way for me to be successful and admired was to always be the smartest person in the room, but God used this moment to teach me that this was a fool's game. My security isn't found in my intelligence or my preparation, but only in the love, forgiveness, and acceptance of God. I began to understand that God had orchestrated all of this for my benefit—He had done His part to expose my faulty Heart Logic and shine a light on the true source of security.

Rewriting Your Heart Logic

You can't cross your gap if the fundamental conclusions you've drawn—about who you are, who God is, who people are, and what this world is—don't align with God's promises. Think about it. Is it possible to adopt a Christ-based identity when you're still convinced that you aren't valuable to God? Is it possible to trust God when things make absolutely no sense if you aren't sure He's got your best interests in mind? Is it possible to let yourself be led by God if you can't trust Him?

If there are too many "nos" to these answers, you may be able to make life work well enough to get by, and you may smile so people assume you're doing fine, but you'll wear a mask to fool people—and maybe fool yourself. And you'll miss out on the greatest adventure of all time: living as God's masterpiece, full of joy, love, and purpose.

When our Heart Logic is rewritten, we say, "Yes, God is good," so we trust Him and surrender to Him. We say, "Yes, I'm good even though I'm flawed," so we walk in grace with security and confidence. We say, "Yes, people have some goodness, even in their brokenness," so we move toward them with wisdom and love. And we say, "Yes, life is good," so we trust God to use everything, the blessings and the heartaches, to accomplish His good purposes.

How can you resolve faulty Heart Logic?

It begins with examination. As we listen to people tell us the stories of their hearts, there often comes a point when we have to look them in the eyes and say things like, "You say you trust God, but I'm not convinced that when things get really tough, you do." Or "You say you believe that people are good, but I'm not convinced that you can trust anyone enough to let him in." We point out the gap between what they believe in their heads and the stories that have been written on their hearts. Awareness is the fuel of change.

At this point, lean into what you've learned about the story of your heart. How have the connected dots led you to conclusions about the Heart Logic questions?

What conclusions have you drawn? And how did you come to these conclusions? What happened in your story that convinced you that God is only good when life is easy? What happened that convinced you that people aren't trustworthy and there's no good in them? What taught you that you're always one step away from being rejected, and you aren't valuable?

A good understanding of your story helps you understand the reasons behind your faulty Heart Logic. This is the first crucial step to untethering yourself from the misguided conclusions!

As you grow and become more secure, you'll want to reevaluate your answers to these questions with the freedom of reason, evidence, and faith instead of the unwanted influence of a Sore Spot. You'll have freedom to decide things like, "People are good, even though they're flawed. That means I can trust wisely."

Being able to say a healthy "yes" to all four Heart Logic questions requires you to be honest about Sore Spots, grieve the losses, forgive those who hurt you, ask for forgiveness for hurting people, and heal the deep wounds that have been untended too long.

It's inevitable that you'll have fears and doubts along the way, but when you've taken ownership of the process, you can keep coming back to the security of God's promises.

Someone told Brennan Manning, "The most urgent need in your life is to trust what you have received."[9] It takes audacious trust to say "yes" to all four questions. As you redeem your Heart Logic and begin to rest in the security that comes from believing in the goodness of God, trust and hope will take root in your heart. Imagine a life fueled by unwavering trust and hope. Envision how it will multiply peace, joy, affection, and contentment. God's beautiful story becomes clearer as you align your Heart Logic with His perspective.

Hand the pen to God so He can edit this piece of the story of your heart.

---

9 Brennan Manning, *Ruthless Trust: A Ragamuffin's Pathway to God*, p. 1.

Reflection

Do any of the three examples of people who wrestled with their answers to the questions ring true for you? If so, explain how you've been affected.

Describe how you internalized your Heart Logic in each of the three phases of your development:

- Early childhood

- When you first trusted Christ

- As you've grown in your faith

At this point, what are your hesitations about entering or continuing the process of God editing your story? (Be honest, everybody has them!)

What difference does it (or would it) make to be able to give a resounding "yes" to all of the Heart Logic questions?

What's your part and what's God's part in your changing your answers?

CHAPTER 7

Private Conclusions and Life Lessons

Above all else, guard your heart, for everything you do flows from it.

—PROVERBS 4:23

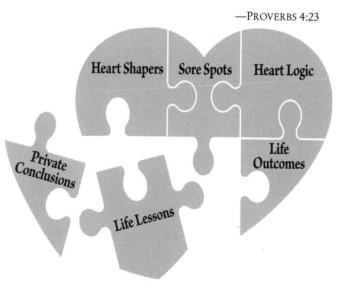

E llen was convinced her feelings didn't matter. Whenever something was hard, she could hear the familiar voice of her mom saying, "Quit complaining! The past is the past. Just move on." Her family provided no room for grief, sadness, or disappointment. The message was loud and clear: "Get over it!" She learned how to push feelings aside and put on a happy face. That was her strategy to cope in her family's culture, and it became her strategy for every relationship.

In her career and her friendships, people often complimented her on her sunny optimism and how she never let things get her down. Their comments reinforced her belief that she really wasn't affected by hardships like other people, perpetuating her self-deception and self-denial. When she married, her husband was amazed that she always looked on the bright side of things. Ellen always wore a smile.

Ellen minimized her feelings, faked a smile, and let the effects of heartaches accumulate. But she was clueless about all this. She thought she was handling life exactly right.

Denial can be powerful and pervasive, but reality can shatter the deception. When Ellen's husband was unexpectedly fired after 20 years with the company, the task of parenting two foster boys with trauma histories and walking through the ongoing stress of limited finances, anger, and criticism crushed her illusions that she had it all together.

Ellen wasn't completely oblivious to the emotional toll of her family circumstances, but she couldn't admit the depth of her fear, self-doubt, frustration, and resentment. These powerful emotions had to come out in some way, and they started leaking out as irritation and criticism. Although she still tried to wear a happy face, she snapped at her foster sons and criticized them for things she used to tolerate. She started villainizing everyone at work, even if they had no part in her husband's firing. Now, rampant pessimism colored her outlook. She knew it was there, but she didn't know why. She was confused. After all, things don't get to her! Or so she thought.

The message written on Ellen's heart ("Get over it.") had created a paradigm for thinking, feeling, and doing, but now, her ability to hold her life together with duct tape and bailing wire was failing badly. She had been proud of the compliments that she could handle anything, so it was especially hard to admit she couldn't. She despised the feeling of weakness. She denied the pain and excused her angry behavior in a desperate attempt to keep from being honest. And now under enormous stress, her old paradigm couldn't save her. Anger, rejection, and fear cut right through it. Without understanding the underlying causes, she was helpless to change it.

In Chapter 1, we talked about how your heart is the gatekeeper of your life, with every other part flowing from it. As you continue to uncover the story of your heart, it's important to understand how it affects every aspect of your life.

The next element in the story is called Private Conclusions, which is your personal set of truths and strategies that have been formed by Heart Shapers, Sore Spots, and Heart Logic. Private Conclusions are the beliefs formed through the filter of your old pain and your strategies to make your way through life in spite of it. The things you think and do aren't random or merely the product of bad habits. They originate in the story written on your heart, and the emotions attached to the story are every bit as important as the cognitive concepts in shaping them.

Your mind is the home to nuanced thinking, understanding, and interpretations. These are your experiential truths acquired through experiences. Your thinking and corresponding emotions guide your responses. Your responses may be your coping mechanisms, methods for achieving, ways of relating to others, the way you engage (or disengage) with your emotions, and so much more.

A flawed story inevitably results in flawed Private Conclusions. For example, if you have a Sore Spot of shame that tells you that you aren't valuable (Heart Logic), you may misinterpret tension in a relationship as entirely your fault. And you may respond by taking the blame for something that wasn't yours to own and over-apologizing. If you have a Sore Spot of pride and someone challenges your opinion, you'll probably feel insulted and outraged, accusing the person of being "out of line." You'll find a way to punish the person so she'll never do it again.

Private Conclusions are private, not because they're meant to be secret, but because they're hidden deep in your soul. You might occasionally recognize them, but often they remain behind the scenes, unarticulated, and unnoticed. Secrecy allows them to exert powerful unseen and unwanted influences. They're also private because they're part of your unique story.

If Private Conclusions go unexamined, they remain unchallenged, leaving you vulnerable to the catalytic forces of Sore Spots and flawed Heart Logic. The longer you live with your existing Private Conclusions, the more you settle into self-defeating ways of thinking and being. Your pathway narrows as you age and develop rigid habits and routines. When these become normalized, you feel more comfortable with your faulty Private Conclusions, even if they keep you stuck in dysfunctional assumptions and unhealthy responses.

Little t truths and small s strategies

Isaiah had an expansive view of God and became his mouthpiece. Through the prophet, God said, "'For my thoughts are not your thoughts, neither are your ways my ways,' declares the LORD. 'As the heavens are higher than the earth, so are my ways higher than your ways and my thoughts than your thoughts'" (Isaiah 55:8-9). This is a warning that we can't always trust our assumptions.

Let's look more deeply at the two elements that make up Private Conclusions: your experiential truth (little t truth) and your personal strategies (small s strategies).

—Little t truths

In Chapters 5 and 6, you looked at your Heart Logic: your basic, fundamental conclusions about people, life, God, and yourself. These conclusions are shaped intuitively, not by deliberation but by experience.

Heart Logic is the deepest level of your understanding and meaning. The primitive conclusions evolve into more defined, articulate, semi-conscious ways of thinking, called your *little t truths*, which are what you believe and the ways you understand life based on your experiences.

Little t truths are more sophisticated and nuanced than Heart Logic. Your questions progress from high-level questions like, "Is God good?" to something more specific like, "How could God let me go through this crushing divorce?" Your experience shapes your meaning and purpose, moving from, "Am I enough?" to "Why doesn't my wife want to spend more time with me?" In answering these nuanced questions, you establish little t truths. You might decide that God stopped caring about you or that your wife has given up on you. These become the truths you hold, the truths you believe above all else, the truths that determine the direction of your life. Little t truths are the meaning you make as part of daily living about things like people's motivations, what experiences mean about you, what success means, and so much more. You may not always notice little t truth running through your head, but it's subtle "voice" is within you. If a Sore Spot and imperfect Heart Logic are guiding you, you're vulnerable to little t truths that don't match God's Truth. That's where you get in trouble.

For example, if Henry's Sore Spot makes him feel unworthy, and his wife gets involved in an emotional affair, his conclusion (little t truth) will likely be that he failed to love her well enough and wasn't worth her affection, when in reality, he has been devoted, attentive, and available. Without the influence of that Sore Spot, he would have seen that his wife's brokenness was responsible for her failure.

Your experience may teach you a truth that lines up with God's perspective. Maybe your family knew how to give grace, teaching you that you aren't the sum of your mistakes—just like God relates to you (1 John 1:9, Psalm 103:12). But often, the lessons we've learned in our families are in tension with God's perspective. Multiple rounds of rejection by friends may have taught you that you aren't worth anyone's time, while God says He delights in you (Zephaniah 3:17, Psalm

147:11). While you may have some elements of little t truth that line up with God's perspective, it's the little t truths *that don't line up* with God's perspective that need our attention!

In the book, *Who Switched Off my Brain?* cognitive neuroscientist, Dr. Caroline Leaf, unpacks the damaging influence of toxic thoughts on our physical, mental, and emotional wholeness. Dr. Leaf's message is clear: "Our toxic thinking is like poison . . . . A thought may seem harmless, but if it becomes toxic, even just a thought can become physically, emotionally, or spiritually dangerous." Dr. Leaf explains that research shows that "as much as 87% to 95% of mental and physical illnesses are a direct result of toxic thinking—proof that our thoughts affect us physically and emotionally."[10]

Little t truths aren't just nuisances. They're dangerous.

We need to know a few other important things about little t truths:

First, holding little t truths doesn't necessarily mean you're ungodly or stupid. It simply means that you've had imperfection written upon your heart because you're a flawed person living in a flawed world.

Second, little t truths are the products of experience—and as we've seen, experience isn't a reliable teacher. Sometimes our perspective of reality is off, like the example of Henry not being able to see that his wife's emotional affair wasn't his personal failure. But of course, we need to be objective so we can assign appropriate responsibility. For instance, Henry may have failed miserably as a husband, and he may have had his own affair. That truth doesn't excuse his wife, but it certainly doesn't exonerate him, either. In this case, Henry would

---

10 Caroline Leaf, *Who Switched Off My Brain?: Controlling Toxic Thoughts and Emotions*, Revised Edition (Nashville: Thomas Nelson, 2009),

shoulder some of the responsibility for the relational problems that led to the affair.

Even when hard realities exist (like Henry falling short as a husband), it still doesn't give them power to define ultimate truth. If Henry sees himself as a failure, God's truth says that grace is available to those who repent and experience His forgiveness (2 Corinthians 12:8-9). Henry has to acknowledge his failure and take steps to become trustworthy again, but he's still a child of God. Even if his wife rejects him, he can depend on God for his identity (Genesis 1:27, John 1:12). So, what *seems* true to you, even if affirmed by others, may not *be* truth.

Third, emotions have power to shape our perceptions (little t truth). In Chapter 3, we saw that Sore Spots influence the formation of little t truths, and Sore Spots are often full of untrustworthy emotions. Jeremiah warns us, "The heart is deceitful above all things and beyond cure. Who can understand it?" (Jeremiah 17:9) Our feelings are distorted and confused because our Sore Spots give us a perceptual bias.

Dr. Leaf also explains how thinking creates emotions. She says, "Your thoughts can sweep away stress, making you more clever, calm, and in control of your emotions, or they can do just the opposite! The choice is yours. Every thought we think should be weighed carefully, because as we think so we are."[11]

The connection between our emotions and little t truths creates a big problem: What feels true isn't always true. The feelings created by our thoughts haven't come from a trustworthy source, but we often give our feelings the power to tell us what's true and right and what to do!

---

11 Ibid.

Some people say they aren't highly emotional and may not have the same degree of feeling tied to their little t truths. However, that doesn't make their little t truths any less convincing and dangerous.

Henry came to the wrong conclusion that he was to blame for his wife's affair, and he suffered the pain and sorrow of believing he was unworthy. As he listened to his wife tell him that she was in love with another man, he felt overwhelming guilt and fear . . . not anger. These powerful emotions reinforced his self-perception of unworthiness, and he felt completely justified in vicious self-condemnation.

It's important to remember that feelings aren't a bad thing to be avoided at all costs. We have to be wise enough to evaluate our feelings and only trust the ones that are tuned in to the Holy Spirit, not the ones that come from the dark places in our heart's story. The Holy Spirit may cause you to feel afraid when you're about to do something incredibly unwise, like lying, drinking too much, or paying too much attention to someone who isn't your spouse. A Sore Spot of fear can cause you to feel terribly afraid even when you have a business opportunity that's well-founded. You need to learn to tell the difference.

Little t truths can't be accepted as law until they're examined in light of God's perspective.

Little t truths for each Sore Spot

Over the years, we've helped thousands of people identify their little t truths. Here are a few examples of little t truths that correspond to the six Sore Spots from Chapter 3:

Shame—*Little t truths:*
- "I'm no better than the worst mistake I've made."
- "God is looking at me as a failure."
- "Not only did I just do something bad, but I *am* bad."

Fear—*Little t truths:*
- "People are just trying to manipulate me, and I can't believe what they say."
- "The world is a very dangerous place, and I know bad things will happen to me."
- "They call it pessimism. I call it realism."

Inadequacy/Insecurity—*Little t truths:*
- "I don't know if I can do it. I don't have what it takes."
- "I'm a small cog in the wheel. I'm insignificant."
- "I'm only as good as my last performance, and it stinks."

Rejection—*Little t truths:*
- "I don't belong. I don't have a place. I'm lonely, and I'll stay that way."
- "No one cares about me."
- "I must be terribly flawed because no one wants to be with me."

Unvalued—*Little t truths:*
- "I'm not important enough to matter to anybody."
- "I'm not worth anyone's attention."

- "I have no skills, talents, or abilities—and everyone knows it."

Pride—*Little t truths:*
- "Other people are idiots. What would they do without me?"
- "Things always work best when they're done my way."
- "My needs are more important than anyone else's."

The Two Gospels Syndrome

Each week I (John) sit in a room with some of the most influential pastors and leaders in the world to listen to their stories. Can you guess what I hear? Little t truths!

Many of these leaders stand on stages each week sold-out to the biblical truths they're teaching, like 2 Corinthians 12:9 which says, "But he said to me, 'My grace is sufficient for you, for my power is made perfect in weakness.' Therefore I will boast all the more gladly about my weaknesses, so that Christ's power may rest on me." But these leaders tell me things like, "I just can't forgive myself for being so critical of my wife all those years." Or "I preach the love of God with all my heart, but to be honest, I have trouble believing it for myself." What's going on? These leaders have a case of the Two Gospels Syndrome. Maybe you do, too.

This syndrome means that you can believe God's Word, convinced of its validity and sold-out to its principles, but you've made yourself an exception to some portion of it. You've come to the conclusion that it can't be true for you. Your flawed life experiences have been more real, tangible, and powerful than the truth of God's Word.

When you believe some portion of God's Word is true for everyone but you, you've become a victim of the Two Gospels Syndrome. Without intending to be blasphemous, I'd say you've tried to rewrite God's Word!

Here's what living with two gospels might look like:

- You might believe that God loves unconditionally, but you hold the little t truth that He's keeping a record of wrongs for you, even after your repentance.
- You may believe that God is in control, yet you still believe the little t truth that it's up to you to fix things when life gets tough.
- You may believe that God offers the gift of free grace and mercy, yet you still believe a little t truth that you're unworthy because you haven't performed well enough.

When the Two Gospels Syndrome is in effect, little t truths are in conflict with Big T Truths—and little t truths are winning, even for the most mature believers.

—Small s strategies

The story written on your heart will also lead you to conclusions about how you should navigate life. When you form little t truths, they inform how you respond to circumstances. This is a fact: Your choices always line up with what you believe to be true. Life strategies based on little t truths are called *small s strategies*.

Remember Ellen in the first part of the chapter? Ellen held the belief that her feelings didn't matter. What was her strategy? She minimized her feelings and faked a smile. Your choices make much more sense when you understand the beliefs behind the behavior.

As with little t truths, your experience may teach you a strategy that lines up with God's will and ways. But often, our small s strategies compete with God's ways. That's where we find ourselves echoing the exasperated words of Paul: "I do not understand what I do. For what I want to do I do not do, but what I hate I do" (Romans 7:15). We find ourselves coping in ways that actually make things worse and leave us frustrated. While some of your small s strategies might reflect God's intentions, it is the small s strategies leading you away from God's pathway that need attention and redemption.

We use small s strategies to try to cover up or cope with the perceived realities based on little t truths. For example, if you believe that people will try to manipulate you (little t truth), your small s strategy might be to withhold trust from all people out of fear, whether they're trustworthy or not. That small s strategy competes with God's intention for us to start from a place of trust and move from it only when it's warranted, so that we live in a loving, supportive community (Galatians 6:2, Romans 12:15). Or if you believe you know what's best (little t truth), you'll probably try to stay in control of everyone everywhere at all times (small s strategy), which competes with your need to surrender and trust (Galatians 2:20, Proverbs 3:5-6).

Dave Monroe had some flawed small s strategies, but they made perfect sense to him. He grew up in a family that expected a lot from him. Whenever he messed up, the phrase he heard was: "Monroes don't do that!" While perhaps well-intended by his parents to help Dave set higher standards for himself, the phrase taught him a little t truth: It's not okay to mess up! He developed a strategy to make himself okay in light of that truth. He hid.

Dave developed a facade of perfection. It was the only view of himself that he permitted others to see. He hid all of his embarrassment, shame, and fear. He was convinced it wasn't safe to let anyone get too close, so people only knew what Dave wanted them to know. That left Dave completely on his own as he tried to fight a battle with pornography. He hid that, too. He'd been introduced to pornography in junior high, and he battled it through college and as he dated his wife. He vowed to be done with it once and for all after getting married soon after they graduated. He figured he wouldn't be tempted if he had sex with his wife, but he wasn't prepared for the pull it continued to have on him, even when his physical relationship with his wife was good.

When he slipped again, the sinking feelings of shame and self-disgust overwhelmed him. To try to get those feelings to go away, Dave used his tried and tested strategy: hide and compartmentalize. He was convinced that he wouldn't be accepted if he was honest and vulnerable with his wife, even though he couldn't articulate this little t truth very clearly. Hiding perpetuated the struggle because problems thrive in the darkness. It took five years of living with massive shame and lying to his wife before Dave found the courage to challenge his small s strategy of hiding. He found the courage to tell his wife...and tell her everything. That moment changed the trajectory for Dave. As soon as he stopped hiding, he could start walking the pathway toward integrity and forgiveness. Breaking the power of a secret was a crucial step that led to him welcoming accountability to keep him honest and healthy.

Examples of Small S Strategies

Over the years, we've helped many people identify the small s strategies getting in the way of thriving. These statements represent the internal voices of the most common small s strategies:

Hide: Be invisible or wear a mask.

1) "Don't stand out."

2) "Don't make waves."

3) "Don't have opinions."

4) "Keep up the right image."

5) "Keep secrets and cover up."

Little t truths behind the strategy: "If nobody notices me, bad things won't happen and negative consequence won't come." "It's not safe to be the real me." "People will judge me if they know me." "Keeping people happy is the only way they'll accept me." "If everyone sees me as perfectly put together, I'll never be challenged or rejected."

Deny: Pretend nothing is wrong.

1) "Just forget about it and move on."

2) "Put on a happy face."

3) "Problem? What problem?"

4) "Minimize your feelings and the situation."

5) "Accept the fact that it's hopeless to look for real solutions."

Little t truths behind the strategy: "Keeping the right image is most important." "Other people have it worse, so what I'm going through doesn't matter." "There's no fixing this, so there's no need to worry about it." "It's best to keep hurt, fear, and anger hidden."

Settle: Accept that this is as good as it gets.

1) "Settle for mediocrity."

2) "Accept the fact that nothing will ever get better."

3) "Give up on yourself, someone else, or the situation."

4) "Lower your standards."

5) "Force yourself to be okay with things that just aren't okay."

Little t truths behind the strategy: "This is all I deserve." "I have it coming because of what I've done." "I don't have it in me to be better than I am." "Nobody believes in me."

Self-sufficiency: Overrely on yourself.

1) "Depend on yourself, be over-prepared, and always have a plan."

2) "Always defend yourself."

3) "Keep risk low by staying in charge."

4) "Don't count on anyone for anything."

5) "Put your walls up with others and protect yourself."

6) "Don't let other people get to you."

Little t truths behind the strategy: "All I have is me." "Other people will just disappoint me." "No one is there for me." "I can't trust others." "God doesn't really care about me." "I don't really need anyone. It's better when I do it myself."

Go numb: Don't risk feeling the weight of reality.

1) "Don't feel anything. Protect yourself from hurt, pain, and heartache."

2) "Shut off your emotions and become overly logical. Live in your head."

3) "Don't pay attention to any emotions inside."

4) "Above all, don't be vulnerable."

5) "Wear a mask."

Little t truths behind the strategy: "If I start to cry or get angry, I won't be able to stop, and that's really scary." "Everything will be better if I just don't feel anything." "I've always got to be ready for the bad that's around the corner." "Feelings are too much to handle." "No one will be there to take care of me if I'm not okay."

Compartmentalize: Separate parts of your life or identity to deal with incongruence.

1) "Create different boxes inside of you to store incongruent information. Do this well, and you can be okay with some pretty horrible things."

2) "Separate your public and private lives, so you can keep secrets."

3) "Separate your hurtful behavior from the rest of your identity. Give other people the same out."

Little t truths behind the strategy: "If I face it, I won't be able to deal with it." "It's okay to have a private life that nobody else knows about. It's not hurting anybody." "I'll be okay as long as no one else knows what I've done."

Achieve: Keep performing and winning to try to feel valuable.

1) "Always succeed. Always beat expectations. Always do better than everyone else."

2) "Seek external validation to cover up the internal void."

3) "Keep achieving to keep the praise coming."

4) "Work harder to try to feel more valuable."

5) "Be a perfectionist. Never settle for mere excellence."

6) "Make sure to win when you play the comparison game."

Little t truths behind the strategy: "I have something to prove because I'm not good enough." "I'm only worthwhile when I'm seen as completely competent in everything I do." "I am only as good as my last performance." "The more I do, the more I'll be loved." "Feeling good about myself depends on how successful I am." "I'm only one move away from losing people's respect."

Control: Keep everything under your influence.

1) "Be in control of everything to shape its outcome the way you think is best."

2) "Dominate and overpower others."

3) "Be three steps ahead of everyone else so you can outmaneuver them."

4) "Always have a plan and manipulate your way into making it happen.

5) Force the outcomes you want when it doesn't look like they'll happen naturally."

6) "Don't be vulnerable. Never depend on others."

7) "Run away or check out when it looks like you won't get the outcome you want."

8) "Always blame somebody else for mistakes or problems."

9) "Read people really well, so you can change your words and behavior to please them."

Little t truths behind the strategy: "Always be in control. That's what good leadership is." "Other people don't know what they're doing. They need me to tell them." "Something bad is bound to happen if I don't manage it all perfectly." "God takes too long to get things done, so I'll just help Him out."

Stay busy: Cover things up with activity.

1) "Fill your life with constant activity, so you don't have to face what's inside you."
2) "Don't slow down."
3) "Take pride in being over-scheduled."
4) "Value doing over being."
5) "Ignore boundaries that protect personal time."

Little t truths behind the strategy: "When I'm really busy, I'm great!" "My feelings will overwhelm me if I ever stop running." "There's no point in dealing with what's inside me. I can't fix it anyway." "It's weak to struggle." "God needs me to contribute, so I can't slow down."

Indulge: Quiet the discomfort with unhealthy ways of soothing.

1) "Self-medicate to feel better."
2) "Over-value short term relief, and ignore the fact that it leads to long-term problems."
3) "Drink too much; take pills you don't need. Use drugs."
4) "Over-indulge in a hobby or a mindless activity."
5) "Cover up the problem with something that numbs you."
6) "Self-soothe in a destructive way that keeps the problem from being addressed."
7) "Ignore consequences."

Little t truths behind the strategy: "I just need to feel good for a while." "I deserve this because I've worked so hard." "Problems will go away if I just ignore them." "There's no way to solve my problem, so I just have to find a way to be okay." "No one can help me." "There's no hope."

Good Things Gone Wrong

On the surface, many small s strategies don't sound bad: work harder, fix a problem, protect yourself. And with the right motivation, under the right conditions, and done to a healthy degree, they're not wrong at all.

But when strategies are driven by a need to compensate for and cover up the pain in our hearts, they're "good things gone wrong." These strategies get in the way of our emotional, spiritual, behavioral, physical, or relational health, and most importantly, they steer us away from what God desires from us. When this happens, they hurt us more than they help us.

Brad walked through the doors of Blessing Ranch Ministries, a victim of his own small s strategy. He's a high-level leader who gets things done and makes sure everything is happening according to plan—his plan. Those are wonderful qualities that make him extremely successful and highly respected by people who work under him.

But there's a shadow side to Brad's get-it-done approach. Too often, he has crossed the line from being a good manager to being a controller. When something wasn't going the way he thought it should go, he'd do anything in his power to redirect the outcome. The problem was that he was doing it according to his agenda, not God's. He was manipulating people, circumstances, and resources to determine the outcome. He was going far beyond good leadership. He was taking the place of God and playing the role of general instead of his rightful spot as lieutenant. People working under him often felt smothered and not trusted.

In our conversations with Brad, we discovered a Sore Spot full of fear behind his behavior, and it wouldn't let him trust people or God. His fear produced little t truths like these: "If things don't end up the way I think they should, I must have failed." And "If God isn't doing anything to fix it, it must be up to me." Those little t truths produced his small s strategy to take control precisely when he needed to trust God's sovereignty over him and his circumstances.

Even though Brad's behavior looked fairly healthy to the outside observer and produced great results for his organization, he needed a revision to his heart's story.

He began to envision a better future: What might happen if he trusted people instead of controlling them? Perhaps God would lead him and the company to a better outcome than he could imagine. Perhaps he could save himself all the grief of forcing things to turn out a certain way and accept God's agenda. Perhaps he would have more internal peace instead of so much anxiety and pressure, and maybe he'd be a better leader, husband, and father.

Surviving to Thriving

Many of your small s strategies were probably developed because they worked for you under certain circumstances, and you concluded, "Why mess with a good thing?" But what once helped you survive often becomes the very thing that prevents you from thriving!

That was true for Sarah. She grew up in a home with a dad with an explosive temper. It wasn't safe for her to be a bouncy, full-of-energy kid. He had a short fuse, and it didn't take long for him to get annoyed and yell at her. It was especially unsafe to do something wrong; he escalated fast and blew up at her.

Sarah concluded that her home wasn't safe, so it was best for her to hide her emotions, her opinions, and her dreams. Being a quiet, good girl helped her survive. If she played by the rules, she stayed under her dad's radar. Life wasn't all that good, but at least she stayed out of his blast zone . . . most of the time.

The role Sarah played as a child followed her into adulthood. She kept being a quiet, good girl in her career and her marriage. It had become her identity. Her little t truth was still, "Don't be yourself. It's not safe." Her small s strategies to follow the rules and please people still made perfect sense to her, and she carried those truths and strategies into every relationship.

As she built a life with her husband, she was consumed with whatever he wanted, what he liked, and being whom she thought he wanted her to be. She couldn't have true intimacy with him since there was no authentic self for her to give. They had pleasant conversations, and there was no conflict, but there wasn't anything of substance between them. She never offered creative ideas, shared her opinions, or expressed more than the most guarded emotions.

But Sarah hit a wall and became depressed. Her small s strategy to be the good girl wasn't working anymore. There's no way to have a thriving partnership when it's built on the identity of only one person. She was stuck with a very surface-level connection in her marriage, and she couldn't see how it could work any other way.

For every time your small s strategy has protected you, there have been 10 times it's held you back! What's the outcome? You try very hard to manage your life, but it leaves you exhausted, frantic, and confused.

Because your small s strategy has worked sometimes, you probably conclude that it's the only way to make life work. It has protected you, earned you some points, or enabled you to intimidate people. It seemed like your "Get Out of Jail" card, but actually, it was keeping you in jail. The skills that worked in the past (even occasionally) are roadblocks to an unhindered life.

Life Lessons: Rules to Live By

Private Conclusions inevitably produce a set of rules to make life work. These Life Lessons seem to be good and right, and actually, they seem unassailable. They take forms that are very familiar: "Always work harder than everyone else." "Love others and be vulnerable no matter how much they hurt you." "Don't make anyone unhappy." "The only one you can trust is yourself." "It's not my fault. In fact, it's never my fault." "Obey the rules, at least when they make sense!" You may articulate your rules in a different way, but all of us have a set of rules as our life's guidebook.

How do we write these rules? You may think it's just because your mother said so. That may be partly true, especially if your mother was not one to be messed with! But the rules you adopt as your guidebook are an accumulation of the Private Conclusions swirling around inside of you.

You have been trying to bring order to all the Private Conclusions flowing through your mind and heart. As you've listened to repeated little t truths speaking the same message, they have created your go-to beliefs. You've used the same small s strategies over and over and you've seen their success compensating for the Sore Spot, so you're convinced they work. You've cemented them as rules for living. Essentially, you've developed a default mode. We call these rules *Life Lessons*.

When Life Lessons are driven by a flawed story, the lessons will be poorly written, too.

Here are a few examples of imperfect Life Lessons:

- "People won't like me, so I can't let anyone see the real me."
- "I'll fail, so I won't try."
- "It could go wrong, so I won't risk anything."
- "My feelings and ideas aren't important, so I'll just be quiet."
- "It's all on the line, so succeed at all costs."
- "Nothing is good, so I just don't engage with projects or people."
- "No one is trustworthy, so I'm keeping my walls up."
- "I'm on my own, so I have to take care of myself."

Little t truth is your momentary understanding, but Life Lessons are deeper, stronger convictions that lead you by default. When others look at you, they see your Life Lessons on display. Life Lessons are broad principles that pull together all the detailed little t truths and small s strategies. For example, maybe you had Private Conclusions like this: "My mom is too busy to talk to me every time I'm upset," "People won't understand when I tell them how I'm feeling," and "Successful people don't get bogged down when things get hard," you might write a Life Lesson that says, "Don't pay attention to how you feel." As these insidious messages flooded your brain day after day and year after year, a theme emerged that became impossible to ignore.

The problem is that Life Lessons don't get you what you want. The Life Lesson "Don't pay attention to your feelings" causes you to stuff your feelings, giving them no healthy outlets. Powerful feelings simmer and then boil so long that they explode in anger or implode in depression. Or perhaps it causes you to carefully maintain emotional distance with people, even those closest to you. Faulty Life Lessons can lead to a host of other consequences, each putting a barrier between you and God's wonderful story for your life.

Life Lessons become absolutes. We hold tight to these lessons as our guideposts and anchors. We seldom evaluate them; we just live by them. Our undeserved loyalty to our faulty Life Lessons keeps us living out Einstein's definition of insanity: "Doing the same things over and over again and expecting a different result."

God Won't Leave You There

Isaiah assures us, "The LORD will guide you always; he will satisfy your needs in a sun-scorched land and will strengthen your frame. You will be like a well-watered garden, like a spring whose waters never fail" (Isaiah 58:11).

The points and concepts we've covered so far in the book may sound incredibly defeating because change looks so difficult, but God is neither intimidated by your problems, nor will He give up on you.

As Max Lucado said, "God loves you just the way you are, but He *refuses* to leave you that way. He wants you to be just like Jesus."[12]

We told Brad's story earlier in the chapter. He was struggling with control. Thankfully, that wasn't the end of the story. God gave him the courage to look at his Sore Spot and begin to trade fear for trust. God opened Brad's eyes to the way he insisted on being in control, and God gave him a deep longing to surrender to Him. Brad spent time reconnecting with the trustworthiness of God to help his heart let go of the fear. With his new perspectives and calmer heart, he could experience a true partnership with God. He started slowing down to ask for God's leading instead of charging ahead. In this new way, Brad plays his appropriate part as a leader while letting God be God! Brad still pursues excellence in all he does, but he doesn't outrun God. He still pushes for good outcomes, but he doesn't manipulate people to make them happen. God turned Brad's unhealthy control into a healthy partnership. Brad's palms turned up.

The transition to a healthy partnership with God took the edge off for Brad. His direct reports immediately noticed the difference and asked him, "What happened to you? Whatever it is, keep it up!" They, too, were able to relax, and it brought out the best in their performances. Brad was able to lead his organization where God wanted it to go (following God's direction for staff changes, giving a chance to some new programs he didn't initially support), and it turned out to be a much smoother road than Brad's previous path. His wound became a new source of genius for him.

---

12 Max Lucado, *Just Like Jesus: A Heart Like His* (Nashville: Thomas Nelson, 2012), p. 3.

God wants to walk with you through the same kind of transformation. In Chapter 8, you'll discover God's process of redeeming the little t truths, small s strategies, and Life Lessons. He'll show you a better way.

Reflection

What little t truths has life taught you?

How do you think they were formed?

What small s strategies have you learned to compensate for the little t truths?

In what ways have they worked well enough that you've continued to use them?

In what ways have they hindered your emotional authenticity, relationships, and vision for your life?

How have your Private Conclusions culminated into specific, ironclad rules of Life Lessons?

This is where the partnership with God gets very specific. What steps do you need to take, and what do you need God to do?

CHAPTER 8

The Truth Will Set You Free

Don't just listen to the Word of Truth and not respond to it,
for that is the essence of self-deception. So always let his Word
become like poetry written and fulfilled by your life!

—JAMES 1:22 (TPT)

Heart Shapers   Sore Spots   Heart Logic

Private Conclusions

Life Outcomes

Life Lessons

A s Jesus washed the disciples' feet, He said to them, "You call me 'Teacher' and 'Lord,' and rightly so, for that is what I am" (John 13:13). Jesus was often called a teacher because only God has the credentials to write the story of your heart. Your little t truths, small s strategies, and Life Lessons can't be tolerated anymore! They've convinced you that they are right and that they make everything okay. But all they do is keep the Sore Spot alive and prevent healing. They keep you stuck in your gap and compromise the strength and beauty in your life. All they do is exhaust you by requiring all of your energy to guard against things that don't need guarding, like letting the outcomes fall where God chooses or letting people see the real you.

God offers a new path with Big T Truth, Big S Strategies, and God Lessons that lead you across your gap into a more abundant life.

Trading little t truth for Big T Truth

Jesus was very clear that He is the source of Truth: "If you hold to my teaching, you are really my disciples. Then you will know the TRUTH and the TRUTH will set you free" (John 8:31b-32 emphasis added).

Truth by definition is singular, so there is only room for one voice of truth: God's. No exceptions.

God's Big T Truth deserves ultimate authority over all of the imperfect lessons of your experiences. The power of pain has tried to steal power from God's Big T Truth, and it has succeeded far too often.

You have all kinds of "good reasons" for coming to your little t truth conclusions. Your experiences—dramatic and ordinary—have taught you to see things the way you do. But God doesn't want to fit into your worldview; He wants to recreate your worldview.

You aren't at the mercy of your unwanted thoughts; you have the power to control them. Dr. Caroline Leaf explains that we have more power than we might think. As she discusses the process of protein synthesis, which is an essential component of memory formation, she writes, "Proteins are made and used to grow new branches to hold your thoughts, a process called protein synthesis. So, if we don't get rid of the thought, we reinforce it. This is quite phenomenal because science is confirming that we can choose to interfere with protein synthesis by our free will. If you say, 'can't' or 'won't,' this is a decision of your free will and will actually cause protein synthesis and changes in the real estate of your brain. Now 'bringing into captivity every thought' (2 Corinthians 10:5, KJV) starts to become a lot more important. Thoughts are constantly remodeled by the 'renewing of your mind.'"[13]

God is calling you to pay more attention to His voice than the voice of past pain. He's calling you to see through His lens. How would the world look different if you looked at it through God's lens? How would your heart feel different if the pain of the past didn't have the power to color the present? Might you have more trust? More hope? More faith?

Dr. Leaf also explains, "... [I]f you change your attitude and determine to apply God's excellent advice not to worry, the hypothalamus

---

13 Dr. Carolyn Leaf, *Who Switched Off My Brain?: Controlling Toxic Thoughts and Emotions*, Revised Edition (Nashville: Thomas Nelson, 2009), p. 175.

will cause the secretion of chemicals that facilitate the feeling of peace, and the rest of the brain will respond by secreting the correct 'formula' of neurotransmitters (chemicals that transmit electrical impulses) for thought building and clear thinking."[14]

Even science tells us something better is waiting for us if we surrender our thoughts to God.

Does God's perspective hold ultimate authority in you? Even if you know God's perspective, does it really rule over you?

We aren't trying to create the expectation that this is a singular moment of surrendering that will instantly change everything. We face an ongoing battle to fight (which we talk about in Chapter 11). The battle begins with staking a claim over Big T Truth and allowing your heart to receive it more and more over time.

The battle is especially fierce for trauma survivors. People who have been physically, emotionally, or sexually abused, victims of violent crimes or catastrophic events, relatives of those who have been murdered or wounded, or service members who have fought in wars have a big hill to climb. The "unwanted thoughts" aren't easily dismissed. They haunt the nights and cloud the days. Professional help, enormous courage, time, and often, medications, are required for the slow, painful process of recovering life and hope.

Big T Truths

Here are some little t truths transformed into Big T Truths.

14 Ibid.

Healed Sore Spot: Righteousness

Examples of Big T Truths:

1) "Grace is strong enough to overcome my worst moments because Christ died for me" (Ephesians 2:8).

2) "God delights in me, even in my weaknesses and imperfections" (Zephaniah 3:17, Psalm 103:12).

3) "Even my worst behavior doesn't define me because I'm a new creation in Christ" (2 Corinthians 5:17).

Healed Sore Spot: Safety

Big T Truths:

1) "I can take God-orchestrated risks because God is trustworthy" (Psalm 9:10, Joshua 1:9).

2) "Bad things can happen, but God is sovereign over them all and uses them for my good and His glory" (Isaiah 46:10, Romans 8:28).

3) "Following God's will and letting Him be in control means that I don't always have to anticipate and prepare for everything that might happen" (Proverbs 3:5-6).

Healed Sore Spot: God-Given Esteem

Big T Truths:

1) "I don't need to have all the talents or intelligence because the Holy Spirit lives in me, making me better than I am" (2 Corinthians 12:9).

2) "I'm a citizen of heaven. God has given me the tools to be the salt and light of the world" (Philippians 3:20, Matthew 5:13-14).

3) "My value isn't dependent on my performance; my performance is simply my service" (Ephesians 2:8-9, Romans 11:6).

Healed Sore Spot: Significance

Big T Truths:

1) "I'm united with God, and I belong in His family" (1 Corinthians 6:17, 1 Corinthians 12:27).

2) "I've been bought with a price, which shows how much God values me" (1 Corinthians 6:19-20).

3) "I've been chosen and given a purpose. God delights in me" (1 Peter 2:9-10, John 15:16, Psalm 147:11, Zephaniah 3:17).

Healed Sore Spot: Cherished

Big T Truths:

1) "God pursues me relentlessly and wants to be with me" (Psalm 139:7-8, Matthew 18:12, James 4:8).

2) "God calls me precious and cares about every detail of my life" (Proverbs 3:15, Ephesians 2:10, Matthew 6:26).

3) "God sees me and knows me intimately" (Psalm 139:13, Genesis 16:13, Hebrews 4:13).

Healed Sore Spot: Humility

Big T Truths:

1) "God knows all, but I don't. He is author of life, and I can submit with joy because I'm sure He knows far better than I" (Psalm 97:9, Revelation 22:13).

2) "I'm called to think of others more than myself and humble myself before them" (Philippians 2:3, Romans 12:16, Ephesians 4:2).

3) "God rejoices when I lay down my needs and desires for the sake of another" (John 15:13, James 4:6, Luke 14:11).

Many of us live as if the only truth is our little t truth, no matter how well versed we are in God's perspective. We push back on Big T Truths, saying things like, "I know God says He'll take care of me, but everything has shown me that I have to take care of myself," or "I know I'm supposed to trust God, but so many people have burned me. It makes no sense to trust anymore!" It's easy to reject (or diminish) God's perspective because it's incongruent with the story written on our heart.

Jo Carr and Imogene Sorely capture the courage needed to take God's hand: "To leave the swaddling warmth of my cocoon, my status quo . . . I'm leery of heights Lord, even your heights."[15]

The fight is very real. We're up against a lifetime of experiential learning and the powerful force of pain. Powerful emotions are embedded in our little t truths, and they have been ingrained in our thoughts for decades! We don't know any other way to think! Doing without their perceived protection feels too scary.

Taking ownership of Big T Truths is not just a matter of hearing God's Word for the first time. Many already know God's perspective through and through, but these truths have to be received in the heart—not just the head. That's why the foundation of redeemed Heart Logic is so critical. Big T Truths won't stick until the Heart Logic questions have been reconciled to God's truth. With that foundation, your worldview can line up with God's Word. Only with a healed heart can you heal your mind.

The process of transcendence depends on the simple but difficult process of trusting God's perspective more than our own. Solomon

---

15 Jo Carr and Imogene Sorely, *Plum Jelly and Stained Glass & Other Prayers* (Nashville: Abingdon Press, 1973), p. 7

instructed us: "Trust in the LORD with all your heart and lean not on your own understanding; in all your ways submit to him, and he will make your paths straight" (Proverbs 3:5-6). Many of us don't just lean on our understanding—it's our crutch, our gurney, our ventilator!

As we face the daunting task of reorienting decades-long patterns of thinking, Dr. Leaf assures us, "Within four days you will feel the effects of changed thinking; within 21 days you will have built a whole new thought pattern, literally, a new circuit in your brain. Though brain change is immediate, the entire process takes time to complete."[16] Prepare to fight the ongoing battle for your thoughts. You'll learn tools for the ongoing battle in Chapter 11. For now, learn how to make the initial transition from little t to Big T.

The Nevertheless Principle

In order to give rightful power to the Big T Truth, we need to learn The Nevertheless Principle, which provides a way of reconciling a difficult reality to God's Word when they don't appear to fit together.

The Nevertheless Principle is an acknowledgment of some minor form of truth (little t truth), while realizing there is a major truth (Big T Truth) that's more relevant and prominent. The Nevertheless Principle takes shape as statements that create a dual reality between two opposing truths and gives ultimate power to God's truth.

Nevertheless is a highly redemptive word because it acknowledges our current thoughts and circumstances but holds fast to God's truth.

The Nevertheless Principle sounds like this:

16 Ibid.

"God didn't bring justice the way I wanted Him to; nevertheless, God cares about this more than I do" (Isaiah 46:4, Psalm 46:10, Psalm 32:8).

"I have messed up so badly and I feel like a screw-up; nevertheless, I'm still valued because of God's sufficient grace" (2 Corinthians 12:9, 2 Corinthians 12:10, 2 Corinthians 3:5).

"My trust was broken multiple times by people I trusted; nevertheless, God will never fail me" (Joshua 21:45, Deuteronomy 7:9).

"Life has been incredibly hard; nevertheless, God is with me in my sorrow and creates purpose in the pain" (John 16:33, John 3:16, Psalm 23:4, Romans 5:2-5).

"I was abused for years; nevertheless, God rescued me from it. In fact, He was in the middle of it with me the whole time, urging me to feel His loving presence" (Psalm 16:11, Psalm 23:4).

There are several major premises of the Nevertheless Principle:

1) *Two truths that seem opposing can both be true.*
The Nevertheless Principle acknowledges the reality of both truths. It's an "eyes wide open" approach. Professor and author James Packer explains that these are "antinomies": two contradictory and

even mutually exclusive statements that are both true, like the fact that light is both a particle and a wave.[17] Similarly, journalist and theologian G. K. Chesterton quipped, "Christianity got over the difficulty of combining furious opposites, by keeping them both, and keeping them both furious."[18]

It may seem like there's no way for the two statements to coexist, but if you ignore God's truth, you'll be stuck in hopelessness. And if you ignore the reality of your circumstances, you'll be stuck in denial. For example, you can't ignore the truth that you suffered years of abuse and claim that God's good always produces obvious blessings. This assumption will create a false perception that God's goodness is derived from the ease of life, and it prevents you from being completely honest about the damage of the abuse. The Nevertheless Principle acknowledges both truths that sound like opposites: "I suffered years of abuse; nevertheless, God is good." It embraces the tragedy, the heartache, the disappointment of life, but it doesn't allow the tragedy or difficulty to change or define God.

2) *God's truth has ultimate power over experiential truth.*

The second major premise of the Nevertheless Principle is that God's truth has ultimate power over experiential truth. God's goodness is inherently more authoritative than our pain. Even in the midst of the most painful circumstances, God was there caring, loving, and even weeping. His comfort was there, bringing goodness. His purpose was in it, bringing goodness. His delight in you was there, assuring

---

17 J. I. Packer, *Evangelism and the Sovereignty of God* (Downers Grove: Inter-Varsity Press, 2008), pp. 23-24.

18 G. K. Chesterton, *The Everyman Chesterton* (New York: Alfred A. Knopf, 2011), p. 343.

you that you're valuable to Him. Big T Truth realities can have the highest value to your heart than anything else since nothing can overpower the Word of God.

3) *"And" can't take the place of nevertheless.*

You have to be careful that you don't substitute *and* in the place of *nevertheless*. It doesn't work the same to say things like, "My dad died when I was six so I never got to know him, and God is good." Or "My wife rejected me by repeatedly giving herself physically to someone other than me, and I am cherished and chosen by God." Using *and* changes the meaning of the sentence and gives equal weight to both parts. It leaves the door open to competition between the truths. Most importantly, using *and* won't have the necessary impact on your heart. Your heart needs to hear *nevertheless* to be reminded of the power of Big T Truth and be soothed of the pain, unrest, confusion, anger, or frustration.

4) *Look for the one that doesn't belong.*

To apply the Nevertheless Principle, you have to look for the anomaly. Did you ever play the "Which One Doesn't Belong?" game as a kid? In that game, you're shown a group of objects, words, shapes, or colors, and you look for one that doesn't match the others. You might see a tiger, a parrot, a dog, and a tree. You have to decide which one doesn't belong. The tree! As you look at the evidence about what truth is, which one doesn't belong? If you saw God as faithful on Monday, Tuesday, Wednesday, and Thursday but not faithful on Friday, which one doesn't belong? Does the one time you couldn't see His purpose and plan overrule the rest of the days? Of course, we can't always simply weigh the balance scales according to the evidence of life to find truth. We have to evaluate according to Scripture to assess which one doesn't belong. Is it hopelessness or hope, anxiety or peace, gratitude or despair? Is it feeling loved and accepted or feeling rejection and shame?

When you find the anomaly, you see where ultimate power belongs. It tells you what evidence (Truth!) must follow the word "Nevertheless." The time you weren't safe doesn't invalidate the overall protection God gives you. Or the one time that you were criticized doesn't invalidate the approval God lavishes on you all day every day. You can acknowledge the anomaly while still valuing the overriding truth.

What the Nevertheless Principle Is Not

The Nevertheless Principle isn't a weak "roll over and take it" approach. It's not giving up and resigning yourself to a life of pain and emptiness. In reality, courage and strength are in the fabric of the Nevertheless Principle. The principle requires courage to face the reality of your circumstance instead of avoiding it, and it requires strength to accept what you don't understand and choose faith.

The Nevertheless Principle doesn't let people off the hook for causing your pain. It doesn't dismiss the intensity of your feelings or take away the damage. And it doesn't allow your circumstances to change your view of God's character.

The Nevertheless Principle doesn't dismiss the fact that you've been hurt before. Maybe you're jaded and you live by the saying, "Fool me once, shame on you. Fool me twice, shame on me." But this principle isn't asking you to trust foolishly. It recognizes where you've been but keeps pointing you back to God's truth. And it's asking you to have the kind of trust that "borders on the heroic."[19]

Without the Nevertheless Principle, you'll stall out, get stuck, and give up. You'll have no way to reconcile the difference between your little t truth and Big T Truth, so you can't move forward, you can't grow, and you certainly can't cross your gap.

Stories of Nevertheless

Tina needed the Nevertheless Principle. She had suffered a lot of tragedies. She was sexually abused as a child in her own bedroom, where she was supposed to feel safe. As an adult, she couldn't shake the feeling of having to be on guard, so she always tried to stay in control of people, herself, and events. She couldn't even sleep with her back toward a door because she lived with a constant terror that something unexpected would happen. In spite of her fear, she found ways to do the normal things like get married, have kids, and hold down a good job. But this nagging sense of dread was always in her.

When Tina's daughter turned 13, she started cutting and making threats about ending her life. That put gas on the fire of Tina's fear! She couldn't find a way to reconcile this ultimate threat with God saying that He was her protector. Bad things had happened to her before—not just bad things, awful things.

Tina's strategy was to assume the role of protector. She was doing all the right things—getting her daughter in counseling, implementing a safety plan, monitoring her closely, and talking openly with

---

19 Manning, *Ruthless Trust*, p. 3.

her daughter—but she remained terrified of losing her daughter. She was convinced she'd never be okay again if her daughter took her life. She concluded that God had let her down—as a child and now as an adult. She simply couldn't imagine God being good, so she refused to deeply trust Him with her daughter's situation.

She later remarked, "The Nevertheless Principle saved my life." She had to lean into the depths of her faith and declare, "My daughter is a suicide risk, I can't fully protect her, and I might lose her; nevertheless, God is good, and He's in control." Her new confidence and security weren't achieved by the power of positive thinking. This was something quite different. She struggled to lay the foundation of trust and hope needed to make that statement. When she could declare her Nevertheless statement with resolve, she began to experience security and peace. Tina's new perspective allowed her to be present and involved with her daughter instead of consumed by fear and the compulsion to fix things. She was the mom her daughter desperately needed.

Dalia needed the Nevertheless Principle, too. After trying to get pregnant for years, she finally learned the good news. She was excited to become a mother. After sharing the news with everyone, and a few months later beginning to plan her first baby shower, she got a devastating diagnosis from her doctor: her child, a son, wasn't going to live. He had a rare condition that wouldn't allow him to survive outside the womb. For the remaining months, she prayed more than she had ever prayed in her life. She prayed that the doctor was wrong, and if he wasn't, that God would heal her little boy. Dalia's heart vacillated between hope and despair.

On the day of the delivery, Dalia tried to tell herself and her husband that God was going to work a miracle. The moment of birth was both thrilling and excruciating. God didn't come through like she hoped. She had only minutes to see her baby's chest move with the breath of life before he was whisked away to heaven. How could she live with the loss of her child?

Dalia was utterly devastated. Hormone-fueled tears flowed like a river. She felt hopeless, helpless, and weak—and she was confused. Her little t truths were the source of her desperate hope that God would do a miracle . . . and her devastation when He didn't come through. She thought, "God doesn't listen like I thought He did," "There's no reason to hope in this life anymore," and "I must have done something horrible to deserve this." Dalia had to learn to say, "My son's death was catastrophic; nevertheless, God is still good, life is good, and I'm loved." She had to reconcile what seemed to be true because of the pain of her life with the truth. Eventually, God's voice became louder and stronger than her doubts. She spent many months grieving the loss, but she didn't grieve alone—she realized that God had lost a Son, too.

Trading small s for Big S Strategies

When Big T Truths reign, they fuel Big S Strategies—which are God's ways. Big S Strategies simply make sense when you see things through the lens of Big T Truths. For example, when you believe that grace is sufficient for your sin or mistake, you'll forgive yourself rather than hold on to self-induced guilt and shame (which is very different from the conviction of the Holy Spirit that assures you of forgiveness and reinforces God's love—see 2 Corinthians 7:8-10).

Big S Strategies have freedom within them, but small s strategies are always tied to small t truths, with the goal of avoiding pain. You don't have to work so hard when you employ Big S strategies because the Holy Spirit gives you direction and strength. You're not consumed with finding ways to numb pain and try to fool people that you're "just fine." You just get to be you, your true self. But replacing small s strategies with Big S ones requires insight, courage, and intentionality.

Let me (John) tell the rest of my story that I started to tell in Chapter 1: I had to let go of what I'd learned my whole life. When I was seven years old, I was playing outside when my mom called me for dinner. I jumped out of the tree I'd been climbing, and my foot landed on a rusty nail that was sticking through a board. My mom cleaned up the wound, but in spite of her best efforts, I developed a serious blood infection. I was sick—so sick that I had to miss the first six weeks of my second-grade school year that began a few days after the accident. For many kids, that might sound like a dream come true, but the implications for me were more far reaching than any seven-year-old would imagine.

While I was out of school, the rest of the students reviewed the reading skills they'd learned the year before but, of course, had forgotten over the summer. Finally, I went back to school—still with a foggy summer brain and without the benefit of the review period—now lagging behind my classmates in every way.

One day soon after I went back, the teacher called on me to read out loud. I stood at my desk and fumbled horribly through the passage. All eyes were on me. The laughter and ridicule pierced my heart.

I was so embarrassed! I felt so dumb! And as a result of that defining moment, I drew a profound conclusion that set the course for my life. I concluded I was stupid, and this became my little t truth.

I had to find a way to make the intense pain of feeling stupid—and being viewed as stupid—go away, so I developed a small s strategy: "Work really hard to be the smartest person in the room ... always." And I did. I graduated a year early from high school with honors. I graduated with a perfect 4.0 in my master's and PhD programs, and I became the COO of a hospital at age 37. All that sounds admirable, doesn't it?

So why was my small s strategy a problem? It kept me from fully depending on God. I was too self-sufficient, trusting that I could always find the answer, that with enough effort I'd be able to solve the problem, and that I could pull it off with enough preparation. My identity was entirely centered on my performance, and I was driven to do everything perfectly. I was missing the essential ability to trust God with the outcomes of my life. The irony is that all of this took place while I passionately loved Jesus! You might ask, "How can that be?" My answer is that little t truths and small s strategies crowd out God's Big T Truth and Big S Strategies. Until we recognize the faulty concepts and strategies and replace them, we'll keep repeating the self-limiting thoughts and behaviors.

God used some shaping circumstances later in my life to bring me face-to-face with the limits of my humanity. God had to change my paradigm for success. He did that by putting me in difficult situations when I didn't have the answers, and couldn't get them. No matter how much I prepared, things didn't work, and I knew my resources weren't enough to achieve success. God's message through all of this was crystal clear: "Now that you've learned that you can't do it on your own, let me show you that I can."

I had to learn how to stop relying on my own competence and instead lean into God's wisdom and power. I gave God the freedom to do it His way, and the weight of always being right and always being a success lifted off my shoulders. It was an incredible relief!

Will Big S Strategies Change the Outcomes?

In some cases, a new Big S Strategy will completely change the outcomes in your life. It will put you on a new trajectory, and you'll see things change all around you. Sarah's life is an example of that.

Remember Sarah? She was the good girl who needed a new strategy because people-pleasing and being a chameleon—changing her words and behavior to please people—wasn't working anymore. Her new strategy was to live vulnerably and confidently. She began showing her true self to others, she gave herself permission to express her own ideas and opinions, and she learned to advocate for herself when people offended her. This strategy looked nothing like being a chameleon! Sarah learned to build her marriage on Big S Strategies—a marriage that could finally grow deeper and stronger and be more fun.

However, in other cases, the outcomes of your life will be unchanged, but the way of arriving at those outcomes will be completely different. That was how it happened in my (John's) life.

I wrestled with feeling stupid for decades, and I tried to compensate and prove myself through my education and career success. Even when I submitted my heart to God's healing process, my life didn't look very different to most people. I was still very successful and competent, and in fact, I was even more successful because God gave me more wisdom than I'd ever had before.

But inside, my world had completely changed. Instead of chasing success to prove that I'm capable, I was motivated to keep knocking it out of the park so that I could serve Jesus more effectively. My continued success came out of a new God-dependency, not self-dependency. As I stood in the security of my significance in Christ, I had nothing more to prove, so my competence became a way to serve instead of a way to prove. Even though my life looked unchanged to outside observers, something significant had happened in me that closed the gaps between self-condemnation and self-acceptance and between self-dependency and God-dependency.

And it can happen for anyone who will join with God.

God's Alternative Big S Strategies

What are the strategies that are based on Big T Truth and bring strength, confidence, and humility? We could list many, but here are the alternative ways of living God gives us to move out of the common little s strategies we discussed in Chapter 7:

1) *Live vulnerably: Hold your head high and live openly and authentically in relationships with people you trust* (James 5:16, Galatians 6:2, 2 Timothy 2:15).
- Let yourself be seen and known.
- Use your voice.

- Confess secrets and bring dark to light.

2) *Face reality: Lean into "grace plus truth" to fully acknowledge your pain and struggles* (John 1:14, Psalm 34:17-18, Psalm 55:22, 1 Peter 5:7).
- Dissolve fear and shame with the wonder of God's grace—a grace that enables vulnerability.
- Be real with yourself about the parts of you that aren't okay.
- Let trusted others know when you're hurting and confused.

3) *Pursue discipleship: Go beyond what's easy and known, and chase after God's purposes* (Hebrews 6:1, Hebrews 5:12-14, Luke 17:5, Isaiah 48:10).
- Strive for greater emotional and spiritual health.
- Match your standards with God's standards.
- Initiate change and keep pursuing something more.
- Dream God-sized dreams.

4) *Depend: Be more God-reliant than self-reliant, and lean on trusted others* (Proverbs 3:5, Psalm 62:5-6, Proverbs 27:17, Galatians 6:2).
- Trust God to show you how.
- Embrace your weaknesses as opportunities for God's glory to be displayed.
- Let others help you.
- Trust others when they show themselves to be trustworthy.

5) *Acknowledge and manage your feelings: Experience life to the fullest*
   (John 10:10, Ecclesiastes 3:4, Romans 12:15, John 11:35).

- Acknowledge and embrace your feelings so God can use them
  to show you the assumptions, right or wrong, underneath
  them.
- Don't fear emotions. Be confident that God will help you
  manage them.
- Consider your emotions along with logic as you assess,
  decide, and conclude.
- Be real about what's in your heart with those you trust.

6) *Integrate: Assimilate all parts of your life into your awareness,*
   identity, and self-image (Proverbs 11:3, 1 John 1:9).

- Be honest with yourself.
- Pay attention to your internal nudges.
- Develop "psychological distance" so you can observe how you
  feel, think, and act, and make any needed corrections.
- Take your mask off, and let people see the real you, trusting
  who you are in Christ.

7) *Simply serve: Rest in your God-given esteem so you can achieve as*
   part of your service, not as a pursuit of personal success (Colossians
   3:23-24, John 7:24, Hebrews 11:6).

- Rest in the security of who you are apart from your
  performance. Embrace your God-given value.
- Let God's smile mean more than the praise of others.

- Celebrate when you've done well. Be satisfied and content with the good.
- Measure success by how faithful you've been, not how much you've produced.

8) *Partner with God: Let God be your leader, trusting that He is capable and good* (John 15:5, Colossians 1:17, 1 Chronicles 29:11-12, Jeremiah 10:23, Isaiah 30:21).
- Don't run ahead of God. Submit and surrender to His leading and promptings.
- Remember your partnership: Do your part, and let God do His.
- Relax and accept the outcomes God has for you, knowing He is always good.
- Be flexible and adaptable.

9) *Abide: Slow down enough to be fully present in all situations* (Matthew 6:34, John 15:10, Psalm 16:11).
- Live with enough margin to allow yourself to put aside the undone and focus on the present moment.
- Create moments of stillness to hear God's whispers.
- Value being with God as well as doing things for Him.
- Let God show you the right things to say "yes" to.

10) *Heal: Let God heal the pain you've tried to cover up, so you can be your true self* (2 Timothy 1:7, Psalm 34:18, 2 Kings 20:5).
- Stop masking the pain, and let God be your healer.

- Replace the quick fix with the ultimate healing.
- Let God's presence in your pain be your source of comfort.
- Develop a plan to manage impulses and temptations, and submit them to God.

Transforming small s to Big S

Now that you know the alternative ways of living, it's time to put the principle of transformation in action. With insight and courage, you can abandon small s strategies and trust that God's ways won't harm you. You may be hurt, even as you implement God's Big S Strategies. But there's a big difference between enduring pain and being harmed. Hebrews 12:11 explains, "No discipline seems pleasant at the time, but painful. Later on, however, it produces a harvest of righteousness and peace for those who have been trained by it."

The bruises on your heart have hurt—the first time they were created and every time someone squeezed them—and you've used your small s strategies to protect yourself. You need assurance that God's ways are safe. In the moment, they probably seem threatening because they're new and you haven't yet developed the skills, but as you practice them, you'll see the benefits of following God's path.

When you begin to look through the lens of God's Big T Truths, your small s strategies won't make sense to you anymore. For example, if you assumed that you were no better than your past (little t truth), it made sense for you to hide the messy parts of you (small s strategy). But when you begin seeing yourself as redeemed and loved (Big T Truth), hiding makes no sense anymore. Why would you need to hide when grace has turned the ashes of the past into beauty (Isaiah 61:3)? When you see yourself through the lens of grace (Big T Truth), it makes sense to confess the truth, hold your head high and give trusted others a front row seat to see the messy parts of you (Big S Strategy). And as the transition takes hold, you'll see a natural outflow of your new ways of thinking in your choices and actions. You don't have to memorize a long list of Big S Strategies to follow! You find yourself doing things differently when there's a new story in your heart.

Following God's path is life's greatest adventure. Take time to dream of what it will be like to live by Big T Truths and Big S Strategies. Life will never be the same.

Which Big S Strategy is God calling you to?

God Lessons

God has some very different guiding lessons for us than the ones that are part of the imperfect story in our hearts. Through His Word, He shows us how to live in freedom. These are called *God Lessons*. Scripture doesn't speak directly into every situation, but God certainly provides guideposts through Scripture that show us the way. Living by God Lessons gives us directions that produce freedom, abundance, and joy.

Here are some examples:

1) "I will live in true community with trusted others
because hiding does no good" (1 John 1:7, Proverbs 17:17, Proverbs 27:17).

2) "I'm going to go for it! Even if I try and fail, I'm still good enough" (John 10:28-29, Romans 8:35-39).

3) "I can relax! God is in control when I'm not" (Proverbs 19:21, Matthew 19:26).

4) "I can be bold. God's truth is in me, so I have something to say" (Deuteronomy 31:6, 2 Peter 1:3).

5) "I will accept my limits because I know I can't earn more love from God" (Ephesians 2:8, Romans 5:8).

6) "I'll never run out of hope because God's goodness is greater than the lows of life" (1 Peter 5:10, Isaiah 40:31).

7) "I won't let fear cripple me, because I trust that God is on my side" (Joshua 1:9, Philippians 4:6-7).

8) "I can take wise risks because God is leading me" (Proverbs 3:5, Deuteronomy 10:12).

Trading Life Lessons for God Lessons is a natural part of being a disciple of Christ. The Holy Spirit uses our decision-making process to give us wisdom, but Life Lessons don't give up very easily because they have felt so real so long. You have a strategic opportunity right now to redeem Life Lessons and replace them with God Lessons. Will you take it? Will you make God's pathway your default mode?

What Life Lessons have you lived by? What God Lessons need to take their place?

A Personalized Message

In order to have power to fuel change, the Big T Truths, Big S Strategies, and God Lessons must feel personal. They must speak into your story and into the places of pain. You need to ask the question, "God, what do you want me to remember about how you see me and how you've called me to live?" You need to hear His voice say things like, "You are cherished, even though you have a failed marriage, because you are mine and I choose you every day." Your heart has to be convinced that these aren't just nice words but they are God's words for you. You also need to remember that God's words have undeniable authority, so as you orient yourself with the new thoughts and ways, use the Scriptures as your firm foundation. Listen to God's inaudible but unmistakable voice, in the Bible and in your heart. Often it takes the absence of noise and internal chaos in times of silence and solitude to experience God's presence. Then, you can hear the whispers of His personal invitation to see exactly who you are through His eyes instead of your own.

You simply can't dismiss His words if they are His personal messages to you. If you think you're the exception who can't have a personal connection with God, you're mistaken. These two ingredients of God's messages—feeling personal and having authority—are essential for the new elements to have the necessary power over your heart and break the barrier between what you know and what you really believe and experience. Then, in order to maintain their influence over your heart, your personal messages must be rehearsed over and over and over again.

Take this opportunity to discover what God's personal messages sound like. Give Him an opportunity to speak His truths and ways over you in a very personal way. Find the words that will carry meaning to your heart.

Read scriptures about who you are. (You have probably identified a number of them as you've read so far, but if you need help, look at 1 Peter 2:9-10, 2 Corinthians 5: 17-21, and Ephesians 1: 3-14).

Go beyond Bible study mode and invite God to be fully present and speak to you.

Listen for God's voice. The voice of the Spirit's whisper and the confirmation of Scripture are as powerful as if you heard an audible voice. What does He say about you? What does He say about your story? What difference do His love, grace, wisdom, and power make in your life? What is He calling you to be and do?

Pull out your journal and jot down a word or phrase that captures what you hear. You don't need to hear a booming voice from heaven. You just need to know your story and listen to God's message to you—and bring the two together.

We want you to find a way to bring all of your insights together in a meaningful way that can really speak to your heart and provide you something you can use as a daily remembrance to center your heart and mind on your new way of living. Over the years, we've seen people approach this in two powerful ways. Decide which might fit you best:

1) String all of your words and phrases together that capture who you are and how you are to live to become a story. Write the story from God's perspective and let it become a personal letter from Him to you. If you choose, use your nickname in the salutation, and sign God's name at the bottom to remind you of God's love and presence. You might sign it *Abba*.

2) Begin similarly by stringing all of your words and phrases together. Now turn the words into a prayer of confession that declares who you are and how you are to live. Prayerfully write this to God as a celebration of and commitment to the new way of living He's called you to. You can use phrases like "I am" and "I will" to cover your prayerful statements with authority and power.

Earlier in the chapter, you read my (John's) story about trying to compensate for feeling stupid. I desperately needed God's personal message about who I am and what He wanted me to do. As I walked through Scripture, God showed His will for me. In response, I wrote a letter, imagining it was written by my Heavenly Father to me. Over the years, I've read this letter more times than I can count. Let this example inspire you. God doesn't have to speak to you in exactly the same way, but let my words show you the power that a personal message can have, and let it remind you of the undeniable authority that comes with it.

Dear John,

You don't have to worry *(Philippians 4:6: "Do not be anxious about anything, but in everything, by prayer and petition, with* *thanksgiving, present your request to God.")* **about looking stupid or being humiliated. You don't have to worry about your lack of strength. Stand in the strength of my might, not your own.** *(Isaiah 40:31: "But those who hope in the Lord will renew their strength. They will soar on wings like eagles; they will run and not grow weary, they will walk and not be faint.") (Psalm 46:1: "God is our refuge and strength, an ever present help in trouble.") (1 Peter 4:11: "If anyone speaks, he should do it as one speaking the very words of God. If anyone serves, he should do it with the strength God provides, so that in all things God may be praised through Jesus Christ. To him be the glory and power forever and ever. Amen.")* **I have called you by name, John,** *(Isaiah 43:1: "But now, this is what the Lord says—he who created you, O Jacob, he who formed you O Israel: 'Fear not, for I have redeemed you; I have called you by name; you are mine.")* **and asked you to join with me in battling for the hearts of Christian leaders.** *(Revelation 2:17: "He who has an ear, let him hear what the Spirit says to the churches. To him who overcomes, I will give some of the hidden manna. I will also give him a white stone with a new name written on it, known only to him who receives it.")* **Trust me,** *(Proverbs 3:5-6: "Trust in the Lord with all your heart and lean not on your own understanding; in all your ways acknowledge him, and he will make your paths straight.")* **not your preparation or competency. Live a life of faith,** *(Hebrews 11:6: "And without faith it is impossible to please God, because anyone who comes to him must believe that he exists and that he rewards* *those who earnestly seek him.")* **not fear.** *(2 Timothy 1:7: "For God did not give us a spirit of timidity, but a spirit of power, of love and of self-discipline, or a sound mind.")* **Depend on me, not yourself.** *(John 15:1-5: "I am the true vine and my Father is the gardener. He cuts off every branch in me that bears no fruit, while every branch that does bear fruit he trims clean so that it will be even more fruitful. You are already clean because of the word I have spoken to you. Remain in me and I will remain in you. No branch can bear fruit by itself; it must remain in the vine. Neither can you bear fruit unless you remain in me. I am the vine and you are the branches. If a man remains in me and I in him, he will bear much fruit; apart from me you can do nothing.")* **Be holy in word and deed.** *(1 Peter 1:15-16: "But just as he who called you is holy, so be holy in all you do, for it is written, be holy for I am holy.")* **Humble yourself before me and others.** *(Isaiah 66:2b: "This is the one I esteem: he who is humble and contrite and trembles at my word.") (Ephesians 4:2-3: "Be completely humble and gentle, be patient bearing with one another in love. Make every effort to keep the unity of the Spirit through the bond of peace.") (James 4:10: "Humble yourself before the Lord and He will lift you up.")* **John, above all, be strong and of good courage as you face different challenges in your life. Don't be disheartened or dismayed, even when you are in over your head, for have not I, the Lord your God, promised that I will be with you wherever you go?** *(Joshua 1:9)*

—YOUR ABBA

Fortifying Your Faith

In Chapter 6 you saw how the resolution of Heart Logic (and healing of Sore Spots that precedes it) ignites a process that leads you toward emotional and spiritual wellness and wholehearted living. Remember that—as a sense of deep security overwhelms your heart—you grow in deep-rooted trust and uncrushable hope.

A measure of these ingredients may have been in your life, but only in healing your Sore Spots and rewriting flawed Heart Logic can you reach levels of trust and hope that may have seemed reserved only for the super-spiritual Christians. Next-level trust and hope lead you into next-level faith, where the Two Gospels Syndrome is gone, and there are no more exceptions!

As Private Conclusions and Life Lessons are transformed, you continue on the journey toward emotional and spiritual wellness and wholehearted living. You begin to develop muscle memory for security, trust, hope, and faith as your thoughts and strategies become aligned with your faith. Then, acting in faith becomes normal. You don't have to muster up the will to take a God-directed risk. After a moment of pushing aside the momentary flood of fear, you find your trust and courage—and you act! You don't have to spend hours of solitude to get your heart aligned with the outcomes God is choosing. You acknowledge your disappointments and losses and then quickly choose to join God on His path.

Each of these words—security, trust, hope, and faith—is fortified as you lean into Big T Truth, Big S Strategies, and God Lessons; then you're on your way to your unhindered life.

A Better Story

As you read the next few chapters, you'll examine how your life has taken on the shape of the story written on your heart.

Look ahead to the unhindered life waiting for you on the other side of your gap. The redemption of your Private Conclusions and Life Lessons will directly impact what's frustrated you every day—your depression, your tense relationship, drinking too much, not being able to keep up with expectations, or whatever it may be. As your heart's story is being rewritten, you can trust that God's love and strength will give Him wisdom to write a truly great story.

Reflection

What are God's Big T Truths that need to take the place of your little t truths?

What are God's Big S Strategies that need to take the place of your small s strategies?

What God Lessons need to take the place of your Life Lessons?

What is your role in replacing little t truths with Big T Truths, and what is your role in replacing little s strategies with Big S Strategies?

Take time now to write a letter from God to you or write a prayer of confession.

CHAPTER 9

Life Outcomes: Your Story from the Outside In

As water reflects the face, so one's life reflects the heart.

—PROVERBS 27:19

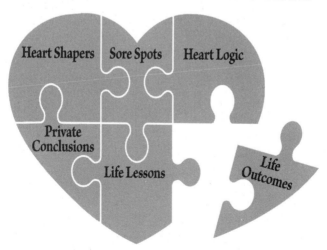

I 'm so depressed that I'm checking out on everyone."
"My wife and I are just roommates."
"I can't stop feeling this sense of pressure on my shoulders all the time."

These are the kinds of things we often hear as the presenting problems in our first meeting with people who come to us for help. They start to tell us the story of their heart from the outside in.

Most people don't come saying they have a Sore Spot or flawed Heart Logic. They don't even realize these things exist. They're looking for a quick fix. They want us to make them feel better and act better, and make it quick! We say, "Not so fast!" By understanding what's going wrong in their lives, we use the clues to work backwards to connect the dots down into the deeper layers of their hearts. As you now know, that's where lasting transformation begins.

As we've seen, the story of your heart writes the story of your life. God wants you to live out the unhindered story He will rewrite if you let Him. He wants you to experience peace (Colossians 3:15), connection (1 Corinthians 1:10), self-discipline (2 Timothy 1:7), and joy (Romans 15:13). And He wants you to make the biggest impact you can make in His name (Matthew 28:19-20).

But when a flawed, and even tragic, story has been written on your heart, you suffer undesirable endings.

Do you remember the gaps in Chapter 1? They are the distance between the life God wants for you and the life you currently live. You might have self-imposed lids on your opportunities—artificial limits that keep you from taking the next step. Your relationships with family, friends, and co-workers might be tense and strained. You might be enduring depression, anxiety, loneliness, or other emotional challenges. You may be overly responsible in some areas (like making excuses for an addict instead of letting him suffer the consequences of his choices) but irresponsible in others (like not being honest about your compulsive fixing and your fear, anger, and shame).

Undesirable Life Outcomes

The unwanted influences of a flawed story show up in six major areas. We'll tell the story of one of our clients as an illustration.

Emotional

When Randal came to us, he admitted he had been a volcano—emotionally dormant for long periods, and then erupting in anger at something that was only a minor annoyance. He was confused and ashamed. He said he had tried for years to keep his anger in check, but as his kids got into high school, his eruptions were happening at shorter intervals.

With an imperfect story written on your heart, your feelings experience the toll. You may find yourself chronically frustrated, depressed, anxious, afraid, lonely, disappointed, ashamed, bitter, or a toxic blend of painful emotions. You may find yourself with over-whelming worry that leaves you defeated and burned out. Or you might feel nothing at all. You long for joy and peace, but they always seem out of reach.

Relational

As you can imagine, Randal's relationships were deeply affected by his outbursts of anger. In the times he put a clamp on his emotions, he had difficulty connecting at a deep level with his wife, and he was emotionally absent from his kids. Then, when he exploded, everyone was terrified. They tried to stay away from him as much as possible.

You may believe you can't trust, so you have to control people and situations. Your control may take many different forms: bullying, blaming, and dominating; fixing, helping, and enabling; or withdrawal, self-pity, and whining. These are just a few examples of the ways we manipulate others instead of loving them. Your relationships may also suffer in other ways. You might not be able to experience relationships as God designed them with ingredients like grace (Ephesians 4:32), compassion (Colossians 3:12), peace (Romans 12:18), kindness (Galatians 5:22), and encouragement (Proverbs 27:17). Your heart might not be equipped for intimacy, keeping you from sharing your highest hopes and deepest fears with others. You may keep putting people down, lashing out, ignoring them, or smothering them with attention and instructions. You might dominate others, preventing healthy collaboration. You might avoid conflict and miss opportunities for resolution, leaving you stuck with a sour taste of resentment.

Spiritual

Randal was a church leader, and he served faithfully. He hoped his wife and kids didn't say too much about the times he was out of control. He made a point of putting on the face of a "put together" Christian when he was around church friends. He studied his Bible regularly, but it was dry. He tried to pray, but God seemed distant. He was deeply discouraged that he had prayed so often and so hard that God would change him, but nothing had changed.

You may develop barriers in your relationship with God. Perhaps your heart won't let you trust (Proverbs 3:5), keeping you from fully surrendering to God. Maybe you aren't convinced that God hears your prayers, so you don't pray, missing out on the irreplaceable power of God (1 John 5:14, Mark 11:24). Perhaps you don't see God as a kind, loving God (Psalm 116:5, John 3:16), putting distance between you. If your relationship with God is compromised, you won't tap into the resources of His love, wisdom, and power.

Behavioral

Randal had no idea where all the anger came from. Sure, his dad was an alcoholic and his mother was passive, but he had been successful in school and in business. His family and friends noticed that he was especially passionate about his college football team. Every play was life or death for him. In every other aspect of life, he was committed to control: his emotions, his reputation, his wife and children, and the people who reported to him at work. He was, as some would say, "a control freak."

You may find yourself doing all kinds of things you wish you didn't do: abusing alcohol or drugs, or using work, sex, or shopping to fill an empty heart and provide some thrills. You may lack self-control (2 Timothy 1:7) and pick up a bad habit that becomes hard to break. You may lack patience (Ephesians 4:2, 1 Corinthians 13:4), and you may bully people or complain to get your way. You may become self-focused and serve yourself rather than others (Galatians 5:13). Perhaps you'll find yourself making bad decisions, giving in to temptation and doing things that once you would never have considered, crossing the line into sin.

Physical

The constant anxiety Randal felt had physiological implications. He had difficulty sleeping, he ground his teeth at night and had to have two crowns, his stomach was often upset, and he suffered from tension headaches. But when people asked how he was feeling, he always responded, "Just fine."

Your physical health may experience harmful impacts. You might spend restless nights without sleep and drag through your days. You eat too much or too little. You're chronically exhausted from the strain of worry, bitterness, and grief. The psychological stress may cause a physical condition to worsen. Perhaps you'll stop caring about your appearance and "let yourself go."

Character

Randal thought he had created the perfect solution to his anger problem: living a secret life. He told people what he thought they needed to hear. He never confided in anyone about the deep hurts and fears that were the product of his childhood stresses, and in fact, he lied to himself by saying all that didn't really matter, and he wasn't affected.

Character flaws come in all sizes and types. On one end of the continuum are racism, xenophobia, and other forms of superiority and hatred. On the other end, we have to look harder, but we find "shading the truth" to get out of trouble, exaggerating to impress, and avoiding telling someone the hard truth because we don't care enough to get involved. While you may do some very good things, under the surface, some parts of your character probably require attention. No matter how much you may want to be a loving person, you aren't willing to sacrifice much of your time, money, or energy to care for others. Perhaps you aren't flexible enough to allow room for others' desires. Your integrity might be compromised because doing what your flesh tells you sounds so much easier than doing what's right. You might see portions of the fruit of the spirit (Galatians 5:22-23) reflected in your character, but not the fullness of all nine as God intended.

The Reinforcing Cycle

A sign in the Australian outback reads, "Choose your rut carefully. You will be in it for the next 400 miles."

Until you rewrite the story of your heart, you'll be stuck in a rut, too. That's because our choices are a self-perpetuating cycle, and until something breaks it, it plays on repeat.

The negative outcomes you experience become a force that reinforces all or parts of the flawed story of your heart. Your painful outcomes falsely confirm that the pain of your Sore Spot is irredeemable, and they affirm your faulty Heart Logic and Private Conclusions.

For example, if your career isn't thriving, the situation seems to validate your Sore Spot of inadequacy. The inadequacy may have led you to play it too safe, lacking confidence that you have what it takes to succeed. Or you may have taken foolish risks. Sore Spots inevitably

cause problems. The experience of disappointment deepens the Sore
Spot of inadequacy and fuels its continued influence, leaving you
stuck in a self-perpetuating and devastating loop.

If the story of your heart includes shame, you probably live with
the morass of painful feelings and secrets buried in your soul—until
you explode in anger like a volcano or implode in hopeless depression. You might be unable to break the hold of pornography because
shame tells you that you can't show your weakness to anyone. As you
struggle on and off for years, you increasingly believe you're worthless, and you can't change. Instead of being honest with someone, you
create elaborate ways to hide your addiction. You have no way out
when you have no one to rely on but yourself. And you end up convinced more than ever that the voice of shame is deserved.

These real outcomes reinforce the imperfect elements of our stories. The more they're validated, the more they remain unchanged.
In this way, the painful story of your heart doesn't have an ending; it
continues, darker and deeper. Without intervention, you'll be stuck in
a repeating pattern. The bruising of the Sore Spot might deepen, your
Heart Logic might grow deeper roots, you might become even more
convinced of your little t truths, your small s strategies will become
ingrained habits, and your Life Lessons will become your only worldview. The result? Your gap remains and even widens.

We need to break the cycle, but it won't happen by trying to change
our life outcomes. The answer isn't a less hectic schedule, more date
nights, quitting a bad habit, or finding a different job. Your problems
will survive those efforts if the roots of the problems aren't addressed.

Breaking the cycle begins in the deepest parts of our hearts. We start with the roots, going down into the depths of the heart to rewrite the story. That's the only way to get out of the rut and put yourself on an upward trajectory!

Putting It All Together

When Randal came through our doors, we started a process of objectivity, healing, and hope. Gradually, he saw more of the trauma he had experienced when he was a child, and gradually, he partnered with God to rewrite his story. He looked at the effects of the hurt and saw the story that had been written on his heart. And then his story was slowly rewritten from the outside in. He was able to identify his family's Heart Shapers, the Sore Spots they caused, his flawed Heart Logic and the Private Conclusions, the Life Lessons and his Life Outcomes. The healing process gave him a new story.

The story of your heart unfolds like the scenes of a movie; each scene builds upon the last, shaping the context and meaning of the coming scenes. What you learned early in the movie influences how you interpret the later scenes. And each scene only makes sense if we understand the previous ones.

It's the same for you: Each element of your story builds on the storyline that has preceded it. Here's how it all fits together: The impacts of imperfect Heart Shapers leave us with Sore Spots. Through the unwanted influence of the Sore Spots and the untrustworthy emotions often attached to them, our hearts use faulty Heart Logic as their foundation. Faulty Private Conclusions are the direct results of flawed

Heart Logic, which then produce distorted Life Lessons, our rules to live by. As we follow this path of imperfection, we try to cope by putting limits on ourselves to avoid or minimize the threat of failure, and we compulsively try to please, prove, or hide to control the people around us. All of this produces painful outcomes, and the process repeats itself over and over again.

The pieces of your heart's story are interdependent. When you don't see the connections, you try piecemeal approaches, and you use rickety bridges to try to get over your gaps. You might dismiss your past and try to fix your present, rejecting the reality that healing your past is the key to a different present and future. You might minimize and say things like, "It's not that big of a deal that I'm still dealing with the pain from my divorce," or "My marriage struggle has nothing to do with the things that happened in my family when I was growing up."

But when you finally see the sweeping, complete story of your heart, you can construct the solid bridge that will take you forward. As you tell the story of your heart, you have to watch for continuity. Make sure your story tracks across all elements. That ensures you're telling the most honest story and gives you powerful awareness.

In the story God edits, His influence has power and authority over your flawed Heart Shapers. You entrust God, not your pain, with the power to shape your heart. As God takes the pen, your Sore Spot is healed, and you can open more room for God in your heart. Your heart says "Yes!" to all four of the Heart Logic questions, leaving you with a platform of security. Your Private Conclusions are transformed into Big T Truths and Big S Strategies, aligning your thoughts with His thoughts and your ways with His ways (Isaiah 55:9).

The following charts show examples of some of the Heart Shapers, Heart Logic, Private Conclusions, and Life Outcomes that might be shaped by Sore Spots. If you struggle with one of the Sore Spots, you may have different particular elements in your life, but these examples will help you connect the dots in your own story.

1) SHAME TO RIGHTEOUSNESS

SHAME—The Hindered Heart

Heart Shapers	- Legalism
	- Culture of no grace
	- Rigid rules of right and wrong
	- Black-and-white thinking
	- Angry parent, caregiver, or someone difficult to please
	- Ongoing sinful patterns
	- A giant defining mistake
Heart Logic	- "I'm not good enough."
little t truths	- "I'm no better than my worst actions."
	- "People wouldn't accept me if they really knew me."

small s strategies	- Hide from people or God.
	- Avoid risks.
	- Become the bad person I think I am.
	- Attempt to handle problems on your own.
	- Keep secrets.
	- Manage your image.
	- Compartmentalize.
	- Stay busy.

Life Outcomes	- Anxious and depressed
	- Self-pity and bitterness
	- No one really knows you
	- Self-medicating behaviors
	- Lack of emotional intimacy with others
	- Stuck in self-destructive behaviors

RIGHTEOUSNESS—The Unhindered Heart

Heart Shapers	- Forgive yourself or accept forgiveness from others.
	- Confess the truth.
	- Receive grace from others.
	- Define identity by God's grace.

Heart Logic   – "I'm good even though I'm flawed."

Big T Truths   – "I'm redeemed from my sins."
                       – "God's grace that is bigger than my sin."
                       – "I can hold my head high and let people see
                         my messiness."
                       – "I'm not defined by others' ridicule,
                         criticism, or abandonment."

Big S Strategies   – Choose openness and vulnerability.
                       – Integrate all parts of self.
                       – Confess the truth.
                       – Lean on trusted others when needed.
                       – Show myself to others.
                       – Be accountable.

Life Outcomes   – Connectedness
                       – Head held high through confidence in God
                       – Bold, yet humble
                       – Intimacy with God
                       – Committed to serve

2) INSECURITY/INADEQUACY TO GOD-GIVEN ESTEEM

INSECURITY/INADEQUACY—The Hindered Heart

Heart Shapers
- Condescending parent
- Comparison or competition culture
- Picked on
- Caregiver didn't communicate value or only praised success
- No opportunities for success
- Naturally shy or socially awkward

Heart Logic
- "I'm not good enough."

little t truths
- "I have nothing to offer."
- "I'm just a follower, not a leader."
- "I'll be rejected if I try to pursue someone romantically."
- "My voice doesn't matter."
- "I'm stupid."

small s strategies
- Achieve. Perform. Win.
- Don't try so you don't fail.
- Allow others to mistreat you, thinking you don't deserve better.
- Act arrogant to cover the insecurity.

- Judge others harshly to feel better.
- Get defensive.
- Criticize self before others can.
- Demand perfection as an attempt to ensure success or praise.

Life Outcomes
- Anxious and depressed
- Unsure in relationships
- Don't let others in because of embarrassment
- Self-critical
- Little success due to little pursuit
- Too much focus on flaws and failures

GOD-GIVEN ESTEEM—The Unhindered Heart

Heart Shapers
- Identity based in Christ
- Accepting God's unconditional love for you
- Define success as faithfulness and obedience

Heart Logic
- "I am enough, even though flawed, because of God's grace and strength in me."

Big T Truths
- "The Holy Spirit makes me more than I am."
- "I have something to say because I know God's truths."
- "Not everyone will reject me. I'm worthy of love."

- "When I speak God's truths, my
  voice matters."
- "I don't have to have all the answers because
  God is working with me."

Big S Strategies	- Strive for excellence and rest in a job well done. - Take reasonable risks, even when there's no guarantee of success. - Expect others to treat you with respect and honor. - Show others your authentic self. - Accept others as they are because there's no competition. - Slow down and be present with people. - Give yourself grace. - Set reasonable and attainable expectations. - Handle ambiguity well.
Life Outcomes	- Security - Confidence - Able to build intimate relationships based on vulnerability - Able to live within your capacity, accepting your limits - Self-acceptance

3) FEAR TO SAFETY

FEAR—The Hindered Heart

Heart Shapers	-Victim of abuse or abandonment
	- Divorced family
	- Unstable home
	- Alcoholic or angry parent
	- Unexpected loss
	- Financial crisis
Heart Logic	- "Life isn't good."
	- "People aren't good."
	- "God isn't always good."
little t truths	- "The worst is going to happen."
	- "The other shoe is going to drop."
	- "People seem to either use me or manipulate me."
	- "I might not be okay."
	- "No one protects me."
	- "I'm walking on eggshells. The people around me are unpredictable. "
small s strategies	- Play it safe. Take no risks.
	- Do what's expected. Follow the rules.

- Be meticulously prepared. Think through all
  possible scenarios.
- Control outcomes, and be one step ahead of
  everyone else.
- Self-medicate to calm anxiety and numb out.
- Stay busy.

Life Outcomes   - Anxious

- Pessimistic
- Can't sleep or sleep too much
- Always on guard
- Live behind walls
- Overly independent
- Controlling in relationships
- Leave others feeling not trusted

SAFETY—The Unhindered Heart

Heart Shapers   - Believe in God's trustworthiness and care.

- Accept that God is in control.
- Acknowledge God's goodness
  and sovereignty.
- See the good in others that God sees.
- Trust God's purpose in the pain.

Heart Logic	- "Life is good."
	- "There is goodness in people, even though they're broken."
	- "God is always good."

Big T Truths	- "The world may not always feel good, but God always is."
	- "It hurt, but you didn't intend to hurt me as much as you did, did you?"
	- "I'll be okay because my loving God is with me."
	- "God has my back and is working upstream for me."

Big S Strategies	- Take wise and optimistic risks.
	- Start with others from a place of trust.
	- Walk in faith.
	- Suffer well. Come out better at the end of hard times.
	- Let God be in control.
	- Let God be your leader.
	- Partner with Him.

Life Outcomes	- Peace
	- Calm
	- Interdependency with others

- Partnership with God
- Healthy optimism

4) REJECTION TO SIGNIFICANCE

REJECTION—The Hindered Heart

Heart Shapers	- Absent or abusive parents
	- Adopted
	- Chronically dumped in relationships
	- Fired
	- Cheated on
	- Spouse is married to a job
	- Moved a lot
	- Bullied
	- Didn't fit in with peers
Heart Logic	- "I'm not good enough."
	- "Other people aren't good."
little t truths	- "Nobody really wants me."
	- "I don't fit in anywhere."
	- "No one gets me."
	- "I'm meant to be alone."
	- "There must be something wrong with me."

small s strategies	- Maintain no boundaries with others.
	- Do anything for acceptance and attention
	- Hide. Isolate. Don't engage.
	- Constantly look for approval.
	- Reject others before they can reject you.
	- Try too hard to win approval.
	- Deny or go numb.
	- By angry and shut people out.
	- Indulge in self-loathing.
Life Outcomes	- Loneliness
	- Self-pity
	- Depression
	- Lack of meaningful relationships
	- Self-criticism
	- Anger

SIGNIFICANCE—The Unhindered Heart

Heart Shapers	- Revel in God's love and pursuit of you.
	- See that God smiles at you, even when others don't.
	- Accept that you have been chosen by God, despite your worst flaws.
	- See the brokenness behind others' rejection of you.

Heart Logic	– "I'm good enough."
	– "People are good, even though they are broken."
Big T Truths	– "God chooses me."
	– "I'm God's child and always have a home with Him."
	– "God sees me and knows me."
	– "God made me for community, but when others aren't there, He's always by my side."
	– "My value isn't dependent on someone else's desire for me or their willingness to honor me."
Big S Strategies	– Establish healthy boundaries.
	– Live with integrity and authenticity in relationships.
	– Engage and pursue connection.
	– Rest in God's pursuit of you.
	– Become an agent of reconciliation.
Life Outcomes	– Connection with God
	– Self-acceptance
	– Contentment
	– Healthy dependency on others
	– Bring out the best in others

5) UNVALUED TO CHERISHED

UNVALUED—The Hindered Heart

Heart Shapers	- Critical parent or emotionally disengaged parent
	- Absent spouse
	- Frequently taken for granted or taken advantage of
	- Emotional and physical needs ignored by others
	- Mistreated at work
	- Others' unreasonable expectations
	- Unanswered prayers
Heart Logic	- "I'm not good enough."
	- "People aren't good."
little t truths	- "I'm not important enough to care about or get to know."
	- "I don't matter."
	- "I'm not worth people's love or attention."
	- "No one can love me the way I need to be loved."

small s strategies   - Do anything for attention.
- Be angry with those who don't value you the
  way they should.
- Stop loving others well who aren't loving
  you well.
- Self-medicate.

Life Outcomes   - Loneliness
- Self-pity
- Anger
- Depression
- Lack of meaningful relationships
- Self-criticism

CHERISHED—The Unhindered Heart

Heart Shapers   - Revel in God's amazing, reckless love
  for you.
- Experience God's constant pursuit of you.
- See others' brokenness behind their
  mistreatment of you.

Heart Logic   - "I'm good enough."
- "Others are good, even though
  they're broken."

Big T Truths	- "God adores me." - "God looks out for my best interests." - "God cares for my every need." - "God sees the efforts I make, even when they go unnoticed by others."
Big S Strategies	- Accept others' limitations in loving well. - Embrace your pain. Let God fill the void by showering you with His love and care. - Love others as Christ would, no matter what you get in return. - Rest in the security of being God's beloved child.
Life Outcomes	- Deep intimacy with God - Filled by God's love even when needs aren't met by others - Contentment - Grace for others who don't honor you well - Self-acceptance

6) PRIDE TO HUMILITY

PRIDE—The Hindered Heart

Heart Shapers	- Acceptance and praise always tied to success
	- Received constant accolades and little critique
	- Lots of early success with little effort
	- Naturally talented
	- Center of attention at home
	- Could do no wrong with parents or teachers
	- Home or church was judgmental of others
Heart Logic	- "I'm very good. In fact, more valuable than anyone else!"
	- "God might be good. But I'm better."
little t truths	- "I'm better than they are."
	- "I know how to do it. They don't."
	- "If they could just think like me, it would be better."
	- "I deserve more opportunities."
	- "What I want is most important."
small s strategies	- Be driven to win.
	- Always be one-up.
	- Be the smartest person in room.

- Be self-sufficient.
- Put others down.
- Judge people harshly.
- Allow grace for yourself, but not for others.
- Be defensive.
- Dismiss feedback from others.
- Control everything and everyone.

Life Outcomes
- Intimidate and offend people
- Tense working relationships
- Spouse feels uncared for
- Lots of success with little fulfillment
- Little meaningful resolution to interpersonal conflict
- Difficulty surrendering to God
- Others feel unseen and unheard

HUMILITY—The Unhindered Heart

Heart Shapers
- Humble yourself before God and submit to His authority.
- Revel in the mightiness of God.
- Accept that your goodness is 100% dependent on God's grace and mercy.
- Connect to the experiences of others.

Heart Logic - "I'm valuable, but only by the grace of God."

Big T Truths - "I'm humbled before the Lord and in awe of His majesty."
- "A team brings out the best in each other; therefore, we accomplish the best results together."
- "I have so much to learn."
- "Every opportunity is a gift from God, not a right."
- "I'm called to lay down my life (and my desires) for others."

Big S Strategies - Let others win or outperform you.
- Work hard, not for the sake of accolades, but to serve God.
- Collaborate with others.
- Encourage and celebrate others' success.
- Be curious about others and compassionate toward them.
- Extend grace to yourself and others.
- Receive feedback and deeply consider it.
- Be flexible and follow others' leads.
- Let God be your leader.

Life Outcomes - Draw others close
- Healthy working relationships

- Spouse feels cared for and cherished
- Healthy interpersonal conflict
- Surrendered and submitted to God as
  your leader

In the next chapter, we'll look more closely at the fight to transform the story of your heart. You'll have put in some effort, but it will be the most productive effort of your life.

Reflection

What outcomes have been compromised in your life?
Emotional:
Relational:
Spiritual:
Behavioral:
Physical:
Character:

Take a few minutes to capture what you're learning about the story of your heart. Put it all together and see the shaping power for your life.

My Hindered Heart:

My Sore Spot:

My Private Conclusions:

Little t truths

Small s strategies

Life Lessons

Life Outcomes:

My Unhindered Heart:

God's Alternative for My Sore Spot:

Redeemed Private Conclusions:

Big T Truths

Big S Strategies

God Lessons

Redeemed Life Outcomes:

By now, you're probably pretty clear about your steps and God's role in your partnership. How have you seen the two different roles play out so far?

CHAPTER 10

Long Obedience in a New Direction

Let me be clear, the Anointed One has set us free—not partially, but completely and wonderfully free! We must always cherish this truth and stubbornly refuse to go back into the bondage of our past.
—GALATIANS 5:1 (TPT)

ugene Peterson wrote a wonderful book about the power of discipline and tenacity called *A Long Obedience in the Same Direction*. But the problem we've surfaced is that we don't want to go in the same direction any longer! We need a new direction. Whether you're making a 180 degree turn or a 45 degree turn, a new trajectory will take you to an unhindered life.

The idea of recapturing God's original story for your heart might sound very refreshing, but it also could sound pretty daunting. You may have no idea where to find the energy to put into your part of the rewrite.

The process of heart transformation *is* hard. But you need to know there's hope, and this isn't naïve hope that just wishes for something better. It's a true hope that's built on a God-designed process for change.

You have to lean into God's edits every day. It will be long and sometimes difficult, but you'll get there if you decide to stay the course.

I know because I've lived it.

Today I (Charity) celebrate freedom from the horrible outcomes from my deeply flawed story. You read about my struggle with insecurity and alcohol in Chapter 1. The story of my heart had to recapture God's beautiful, original story so that I could sit here writing this book today.

In Chapter 1, I identified a few of my Heart Shapers that created a Sore Spot of insecurity. I was pretty confident I was going to win as long as I was on the starting block of a swimming race, but I was sure I was going to lose if I ever showed my heart to anyone.

I had little t truths like, "Keep people happy, so they'll like you," and "It's never okay to disappoint someone." I learned small s strategies so I could live according to these little t truths: "Hide what you don't think is acceptable about you," "Don't show your mistakes, especially to your parents," "Avoid and ignore your feelings because shame is too uncomfortable," and "Keep up the right image in front of people."

One of the most detrimental impacts of the way I learned to live was to medicate my pain with alcohol. That may sound like a cliché, but most clichés have some truth to them. Even though I didn't spend every day utterly overwhelmed by my pain, it was there. The constant nag of "I don't know what I'm doing," "I really need people to like me," and "It's not okay to fail," eventually caused me to use alcohol to quiet those whispers.

My parents have said "Big as the sky" to me ever since I was little to represent the unending and unconditional love they have for me. So many people only wish they had that kind of love from their families. They're sure that if they did, it'd be enough to heal any wound and fill any hole inside them. But even the constant, overwhelming assurance I had from my parents wasn't enough to heal my Sore Spot. Only God could do that.

Eventually, God got my attention and amplified the work He'd been trying to do for a long time to rewrite my story. But I needed to give Him access to the deepest parts of me. First, the foundations of insecurity needed to be deconstructed and replaced with the security found only in God's grace. He wanted me to hear that I'm bold because He lives in me (John 14:23, 2 Corinthians 12:9). That profound truth began redeeming my Sore Spot, taking the pain away and healing the wounds of shame and self-condemnation. It reshaped my Heart Logic, helping me say, "Yes, God, you've made me good and valuable."

For me to become bold, several other things had to happen. I had to stop harshly judging my personality and embrace my introverted self, seeing that my nature had given me a tender heart for others, an ability to listen well, and the capacity to help others feel seen and known.

I also had to forgive myself for the sins and mistakes that brought me shame—the alcohol, the lies that came with it, hiding from people, the secrets, and more. I couldn't ignore these things anymore. I had to stop denying and compartmentalizing so I could face the ugly parts of me. Being brutally honest about my brokenness was necessary for me to experience the wonder of God's forgiveness.

I had to stop letting my value come from the approval of others. I needed to claim the Big T Truth that my right standing with God is what defines my value, not the approval of people (1 John 3:1, Proverbs 29:25). I had to start visualizing God as my "audience of One." I imagined Him standing alone, cheering me on, and being my guide, my shield, and my rock. In *Rising Strong*, Brené Brown observes, "When we become defined by what people think, we lose *our* willingness to be vulnerable. Our job is to figure out whose opinions really matter and ignore the cheap seats."

God taught me how to be vulnerable. I challenged myself to sit in my own discomfort and open my mouth. I learned to quiet the waves of embarrassment and listen closely to His reminders of my value and His grace. I learned that my Big T Truths are marvelously true!

God challenged me to be accountable to a group of ladies and give others a voice in my life. He taught me how to share my mistakes and still hold my head high as I embraced my Big T Truths about grace. When God convinced me of my security, I could receive the message my parents were trying to send me my whole life: I'm accepted in my mess and loved through it completely.

In Christ, I found my security, and finally, I could be seen—the flawed and the forgiven. He also taught me how to see myself as someone who has something to say because the Holy Spirit dwells in me. When I found my security, I found my voice, too.

My story now sounds like this: I'm valuable; I'm good enough (Ephesians 1:7, Psalm 139:14). I don't have to be someone I'm not. I don't have to be just like my mom or my dad or anyone else because I'm God's creation—my shyness, the struggle with alcohol, and my strengths, too (Ephesians 3:12). I don't have to impress everyone and keep them happy. I just have to please God, and it's easy to make Him smile (Zephaniah 3:17, 1 John 4:8, Mark 12:30-32). With a repentant heart, I'm cleansed from all unrighteousness (1 John 1:9). He has turned my crimson sins white as snow (Isaiah 1:18). Therefore, I'll be bold and use my voice to speak into the hearts of God's people, according to His unique purposes for me (2 Corinthians 3:12, Joshua 1:9, Jeremiah 29:11). I will step out of the shadow of my parents and their legacy (where I've always felt the safest) and join God to continually discover ways He wants me to serve. I won't hold back because I remember that the Holy Spirit lives in me, and I can rely on His strength and wisdom as I join God on the mission He's given me (Jeremiah 1:9, Isaiah 61:1-2).

Those are the Big T Truths and Big S Strategies I claimed for my heart. On the days they were hard to believe, I had to tune back into God's voice to hear His sweet words tell me once again that I'm bold and forgiven. I had to rehearse them over and over until they became more real than my old Private Conclusions and until they became so familiar they turned into God Lessons—so ingrained that they could become my new default.

I couldn't do this on my own. I needed the love and power of Almighty God to transform the deepest parts of my heart. It wasn't just about changing a bad habit or two. It was about honesty, insight, support, and the courage to welcome His light into my darkness. It took years to create the mess in my heart, but it didn't take that long for God to do His redeeming work to change me from the inside out. With a foundation of security and righteousness, I created guardrails to protect me from falling back into the trap of alcohol, lying, crippling shame, and the compulsion to please people. And God gave me some trusted friends who didn't laugh, condemn, or run away when I told them about the mess I'd created. With them, I could be me and trust God to continue to rewrite my story.

Without the shift to a long obedience in a new direction, the last few years of my life wouldn't have happened. My dad turned the leadership of Blessing Ranch Ministries over to me in 2017. That was a day I didn't see coming and would never have asked for. But because I could step beyond my flawed story and trust that God writes a far better story, I could put my self-doubts in their place and say, "Yes, God, I'll step into this unfamiliar place of leadership. I have much to learn, but I know you're with me."

As I write these paragraphs, little t truths are trying to draw me back in. A little piece of me is afraid of what you'll think of this book, and of course, of me. The voice of insecurity tells me to hide the part about my struggle with alcohol. A piece of me is afraid that you'll look at me differently when you know—and maybe some of you will. Nevertheless, God has redeemed me and calls me His treasure. The beauty now is that the old voice of insecurity doesn't overpower God's voice of truth to make a home in my heart anymore. I fight back.

From time to time, I still have to fight the battle with my old story. It tries to catch me—in the moment when a highly successful pastor of a church of 20,000 sits in the chair across from me and expects me to speak into his life, in the moment when I'm challenged to speak in front of a crowd, and in the moment when God prompts me to share my deepest wounds to help someone else. The old little t truths try to convince me that I don't know what I'm doing or that I have nothing significant to say. But I deliberately give Big T Truth power over them because I'm committed to not let the old influences steal the holy boldness God has given me. No matter how tempted I may be to go back to the old ways, I'll stay the course and fight the battle for the new story God is writing on my heart. And because of Him, there's a light in my eyes and a light in my life that wasn't there before.

The Pathway Before You

While you understand the story of your heart, you now know that it's possible to believe the truth but stay stuck because ungrieved wounds and unforgiven sins keep you shackled to the past. When you grasp the power of the past, the struggles in the present make a lot more sense. I hope this process has helped you ask questions you didn't know to ask and look beyond the symptoms to the roots. I hope you see a pathway to understand yourself from the inside out.

I hope that you feel a greater sense of hope, even if nothing has changed inside of you yet. You now have language for all the barriers that once were hidden and unnamed. You know how to connect the dots and see the threads among the seemingly disconnected pieces of your life. You know how to call out your Sore Spot, your faulty Heart Logic, your little t truths, small s solutions, and Life Lessons and bring all of them into light. And now you see the specific targets—God's alternatives. Your understanding has power!

Alan Ahlgrim says, "Heart work is hard work." God is calling you to fight the battle for your heart. He's inviting you to take His hand and go deep into the redemption process. He knows this will take tenacity and the hard work of entering your pain, overcoming the barriers between your head and your heart, taking the power back because you'd given it away, and fighting the mental battle so that God's perspectives will reign.

When God's story becomes your story, you'll experience security, peace, trust, hope, faith, and belonging. The best of you will show up, and you will make the impact only you can make on the world. That's the full glory of God's edits in your story.

Towards an Unhindered Life

With our best intentions but a faulty grasp of what's inside us, we've been radically committed to "a long obedience in the same direction," but now, it's time for a change. A long obedience in the same direction is precisely what got you where you are today. Following the same direction means continuing to live out of the old, flawed story of your heart. It's time to embrace a *new* direction. That's the battle before you.

Rewriting the story of your heart changes the direction of your life. As God edits your story, the things that made sense before won't make sense anymore. Your goals change, your sense of purpose alters course, and you flame with a passion to make a difference!

Gradually, you become more of your spiritual self instead of your natural self. Your natural self follows the lead of experiential learnings. It might get some things right, but it gets too much wrong. Your spiritual self goes beyond what comes easily and does what's good, noble, and godly. Your spiritual self is the most authentic version of you because it's becoming who God intended you to be!

Your new direction is a better direction because it's God's direction.

The Unknown

When you ask people what they're afraid of, you might hear things like heights, spiders, or flying. But there's something else most of us are afraid of: the unknown. A research study in 2016 found that "uncertainty is more stressful than predictable negative consequences." We are more afraid of what we don't know than what we do know, even when what we know is bad!

The new story for your heart is unknown, and that makes it scary. We're scared to abandon what's known and comfortable.

The old story of your heart has felt as comfortable and attractive as your favorite book. You know it by heart and you can recite the arc of the story without even seeing the words on the page. But the new story of your heart feels like a new book you've never read.

The binding feels stiff, and you're not familiar with anything in it. You don't even know if you're going to like it.

Courage calls us to choose discomfort because it's the only way to experience the story God is writing for us.

As you try to embrace the new story, something in you may try to convince you that a new story just can't be as good. You might be tempted to pick up the old story again to go back to the comfort of what you've known.

As you and God partner to rewrite your story, He may have to keep bringing you back to the new direction. His corrections are a form of discipline. As we've seen, the writer to the Hebrews explains: "No discipline seems pleasant at the time, but painful. Later on, however, it produces a harvest of righteousness and peace for those who have been trained by it" (Hebrews 12:11). The beginning of the rewrite seems awkward and unpleasant. After all, many of the things we thought were true we're learning are false, and the things we didn't know are true are calling us to radical transformation!

At this point in the process, we need at least one person who has been down this road before us to walk with us. This person—a counselor, a mentor, a sponsor in a support group, or a special friend—will give us insights when we're confused, direction when we drift off course, and courage when we want to give up. We're wounded in relationships, and we're healed in relationships. Don't try to go it alone.

Prepare for discomfort in the unknown new direction, and trust that there's a new story of strength and beauty for you to discover. (We're pretty sure it'll become your new favorite!)

The Long Obedience

When you've been living with chest pain from heart disease, your trajectory can begin to change when your condition is diagnosed correctly. Until then, you survive by taking pain-killers. Similarly, the first step in finding freedom for your heart is to correctly diagnose its condition by looking beyond the symptoms at the roots. We've spent several chapters diagnosing the problem, and we've given you a prescription. But will it work?

You don't know until you try. Will you face the unknown? Will you trust that the "Great Physician" will heal your wounds, strengthen your weak spots, and help you stand strong? You can be sure God will do His part because He's already gone to the farthest reaches to prove His love for you. But will you do your part? We've challenged the myths and arguments that keep you from choosing to fight. Now (if you haven't already), it's time to fight your heart condition!

The right diagnosis points you toward the appropriate treatment plan that restores health. If you have a severe heart disease, the treatment may include undergoing surgery. You may need to stay in the Intensive Care Unit (ICU) until you get stronger. Rewriting your story is like heart surgery—a spiritual process of inside-out change. Your heart goes through surgery as Sore Spots, Heart Logic, Private Conclusions, and Life Lessons are exposed, challenged, and replaced. That's how your heart heals from its disease. A successful surgery means that God's story of strength and beauty is being written in your heart.

Once you've done the hard work to hand the pen to God for Him to edit your story, you'll have a new freedom. You'll exercise your faith more boldly, you'll have more wisdom about trusting people, you'll find your true sense of purpose, and you'll feel closer to God. Your heart will be filled with gratitude for God's amazing gifts. But transformation doesn't end when a heart is changed.

As a post-operation patient, you step down from the ICU into a general hospital unit where you continue to receive medical care. You're required to take your medicine regularly and participate in rehab. Similarly, when God's story has begun to be rewritten, your heart can come out of the ICU. Just like the medical patient, your gains are real, yet they're fragile. You'll need to keep investing in your progress in those early weeks and months to gain strength. The investment is necessary to engrave God's story on your heart so that it will become indelible.

When you finally go home after your hospital stay, you go with an aftercare plan to keep your physical heart healthy. If you stop eating the heart-healthy foods, exercising, and taking the meds your doctor prescribed, you might be back in the hospital before too long. Likewise, the new story in your heart needs to be cared for and continually protected. When you get beyond the excitement of a moment of discovery and life settles back into the mundane, the real test begins. The ingredients for your aftercare plan will come together in Chapter 11.

The excitement and relief you feel as the new story takes root in your heart may carry you for a while in the new direction, but you can't rely on that to sustain you forever. As Alan Ahlgrim said, "Momentum has a one-week shelf life." It takes intentional effort to protect you from leaning back into the old story. It may sound like bad news to many of you who are fixers and just want the job done, but the battle doesn't end when the story is rewritten!

Transformation requires a long obedience. It's a process, not just a moment. It's an ongoing mission of staying the course and holding on to the story God is writing for you.

The Resistance

Expect resistance as you grow beyond the old story. Your heart remembers the pain more than it has hope in something new, so doubt is a constant reality in the early stages of change. The new seems threatening; it seems much better to play it safe.

Things like little t truths and faulty Heart Logic make sense because they are consistent with everything you've believed throughout your life. Your heart reminds you of all the times something didn't fit the Big T Truth! It tries to persuade you that Big T Truth is too good to be true. It says things like, "It's a set up! Don't go there. Don't you remember what happened when you were honest about your pain last time? You may not remember how much it hurt, but I do!" It tells you that it's dangerous to try Big S Strategies like trust, vulnerability, extending grace, and letting your guard down.

Don't let the pleadings of your heart stop you from rewriting the old story. Though sometimes it'll be right about the risk of getting hurt again, it's wrong that you'll be alone and you'll be devastated. Reject the lens that only sees threats. Use this question as your guide: Is this challenge part of God's beautiful story for me? If the answer is "no," then it's right to resist. But if the answer is "yes," the right action is to overcome your internal resistance.

Eventually, you'll be able to relax and feel safe. You'll be able to take a deep breath and say, "This is far better!"

Are You Convinced?

You won't have a long obedience in a new direction unless you're deeply convinced of the value of the new story. You may believe that this all sounds like a great idea, but are you convinced that it's time for you to take action? If you aren't convinced, you'll just fall back into your gap.

We can't be convinced for you. You spouse can't be convinced for you. Your mom can't be convinced for you. You have to be convinced for yourself.

Being convinced happens on two levels: first, by owning the fact that your old story hasn't worked as well as you've tried to tell yourself, and second, by believing that God's way is far better. Are you convinced that there's more in you ready to be unleashed if you hand the pen to God and let Him rewrite your story? Are you convinced that God's story is worth the effort? Yes, it will be hard, and yes, you'll want to bail from time to time, but if you believe the results are worth it, you'll find a way to keep going. There are no promises of an easy life on the other side, but you'll be more aligned with God's will and ways, and that's far better than trying to dodge your Sore Spot all day every day.

Are you convinced? Really?

Reflection

How is your life's trajectory already changing due to the self-awareness you are developing?

What are concrete decisions you've made and steps you've taken, and how has God revealed Himself in love and power?

Describe the correlation between heart surgery and the work we have to do in our hearts:

- What are the signs that surgery is needed?

- Why can't we fix it ourselves?

- What are the stages of healing and recovery?

Are you prepared to face internal resistance? How will you deal with the discouragement the enemy wants you to embrace when resistance comes and it feels hard?

Reflect on the concept of the long obedience in a new direction. Are you convinced that's what you want? Explain your answer.

CHAPTER 11

Fighting the Battle

Be prepared. You're up against far more than you can handle on your own. Take all the help you can get, every weapon God has issued, so that when it's all over but the shouting you'll still be on your feet.

—EPHESIANS 6:13 (MSG)

As we've shared the principles and processes with thousands of people over the years we hear a recurring refrain: "I'm excited." They see the promise of a new direction, but some walk away and fail to do the follow-through that actually creates a new way of living. Especially when things start to feel a little better and they see some early successes, they soon forget that they have to fight the battle for their new direction, or they let up too soon.

You're in a battle between the two stories: the one your experiences have written and the one God is rewriting. It's the battle to trust the right author—your imperfect life or your perfect God. If you don't fight the ongoing battle through targeted self-disciplines, all the self-discovery and inspiration you've found will disappear in your not-so-distant future.

At the risk of sounding a bit discouraging, we can tell you that you're actually fighting two battles: one with the enemy within and the other the enemy without. The war inside you is the one we've described in these pages: Everything in you says that your little t truth is absolute and God's Big T Truth is too good to be true. But as you fight to replace lies with truth, you also hear the devil's whispers: "This is all you're ever going to be," "You'll never be free," and "This isn't really what you want anyway." And Satan uses our own inner voices, so he sounds even more convincing. We desperately need God's truth, but also, His strategy. Jesus invited the disciples, "Walk with me and work with me—watch how I do it" (Matthew 11:29, MSG). God is the general, and He says to us, "Trust me, and we'll get through this together." As His lieutenants, our orders are to take all the help He gives us and follow His commands.

It won't work to just say, "I'll be better someday," or "I'll do better tomorrow." Fatalism feels right and justified, but it keeps you shackled in the darkness of the past. You aren't defenseless. God has given you powerful weapons for the fight (Ephesians 6:13, MSG).

The weapons have to be on target, or they won't be effective. They have to hit the center of your heart, speaking to the pain and lies that keep the old story alive. We need more than wishes; we need workable wartime strategies.

The most powerful weapon is the Word of God. We find descriptions of its power not only in Ephesians, but also in many other passages. Here are a few:

"God's Word is an indispensable weapon" (Ephesians 6:17b, MSG).

"Do not conform to the pattern of this world, but be transformed by the renewing of your mind. Then you will be able to test and approve what God's will is—his good, pleasing and perfect will" (Romans 12:2).

"We demolish arguments and every pretension that sets itself up against the knowledge of God, and we take captive every thought to make it obedient to Christ" (2 Corinthians 10:5).

"Set your minds on things above, not on earthly things" (Colossians 3:2).

"You were taught, with regard to your former way of life, to put off your old self, which is being corrupted by its deceitful desires; to be made new in the attitude of your minds; and to put on the new self, created to be like God in true righteousness and holiness" (Ephesians 4:22-24).

"Trust in the Lord with all your heart and lean not on your own understanding" (Proverbs 3:5).

"For my thoughts are not your thoughts, neither are your ways my ways," declares the Lord. "As the heavens are higher than the earth, so are my ways higher than your ways and my thoughts than your thoughts" (Isaiah 55:8-9).

The Scriptures have the power to expose lies and weakness, but also to instill truth and courage. With the truth of God planted in our hearts (not just our heads), we choose to say "yes" to the new direction and "no" to the old.

Every choice between our flawed story and the new one God is editing is a collision of mind, heart, and will.

Moments of Collision

When I (Charity) got my driver's license, I had a couple of collisions—one with a fence post and another with the rear end of another car. Neither was expected and neither was very pleasant, but they were part of learning to drive. In the same way, as you move in your new direction, you'll experience collisions. They'll feel shocking and unpleasant, but they're part of the learning curve.

Collisions are the moments when your new story smashes into your old one. They happen when a little t truth collides with a Big T Truth or a small s strategy collides with a Big S Strategy. There are two kinds of collisions: recognized and unrecognized. Recognized collisions are the moments when you notice your old, flawed story being triggered. Something happens that floods you with the familiar feelings of fear or insecurity or rejection, and they catch your attention. You start to notice the pull toward the little s strategies that used to get you through (or so you thought). Unrecognized collisions are moments of internal war that you don't even notice because the old ways are so familiar that you don't even realize they've taken root again. You might not notice until hours or days down the road when you've been so numbed out that your wife gets fed up enough to complain, or you get caught in a lie you told to avoid your shame. As you follow the path of growth and healing, you'll gain more capacity to notice the collisions and gain the freedom to battle them well.

Collisions are critical moments! In these collisions, you have the opportunity to choose which way to go.

Will you go back to the old direction, or will you keep choosing the new direction?

To prepare for the inevitable collisions, adopt these strategies:

Expect them.

When you encounter a known collision, don't freak out! Welcome it! Collisions aren't a sign that you're off track; they're probably signs you're charting a new course—a better course. And they don't mean you haven't made progress. Quite the opposite. You're facing new challenges with every step you take.

God uses collisions in a purposeful way, primarily to draw us more deeply into the healing process. Without collisions, we keep going the wrong way.

If you anticipate collisions, you'll be ready for them.

Embrace them.

Use collisions to learn. Collisions are opportunities for growth because they give you clear choices. Don't miss the chance to see where you still need some work, where your Private Conclusions are still holding on or the Sore Spot is trying to resurface. Don't ignore or resist collisions; instead, embrace them.

Use collisions to learn more about yourself. Put your palms up and ask, "God, what are you teaching me?" He'll show you—not to condemn you, but to help you take steps forward.

Collisions are an irreplaceable source of information about your alternatives. They become your friends because they give you opportunities to change the plot line of your story.

Reset your direction.

Choose wisely in a collision. It's your chance to bring things into alignment. After a collision, reset your path in two ways. First, reclaim ownership over the ground you've already gained. Henry Nouwen encourages us, "Sometimes little things build up and make you lose ground for a moment. Fatigue, a seemingly cold remark, someone's inability to hear you . . . can make you feel like you are right back where you started. But try to think about it instead as being pulled off the road for a while. When you return to the road, you return to the place where you left it, not to where you started."[20] Don't let the discomfort of collisions convince you that all is lost. The ground you gained still belongs to you. Just reclaim it.

Second, let collisions adjust your trajectory so that it aligns more closely with God's story for your heart. Learn to see every collision as a God-ordained moment of revelation that calls your attention to the next step in the healing process.

---

20 Henry Nouwen, *The Inner Voice of Love: A Journey Through Anguish to Freedom* (New York: Doubleday, 1996), p. 38.

Opportunities for Growth

Bridget had to learn to use her collisions as opportunities for growth. She came to Blessing Ranch a few years ago, and I (Charity) have had the privilege of cheering her on as she has navigated several collisions over the years. The beginning, though, wasn't what she expected. When she finished her week of intensive counseling, she wanted the process to be over, with no more struggles. She had no interest in an ongoing, messy process of healing. She had too much to get done to be bogged down with more attention to her Sore Spots. I explained (many times) that healing is a process. Finally, after many conversations, she understood and accepted the reality that she wasn't finished yet.

One day, she realized she couldn't ignore the pain any longer. She ran into some friends who knew her from the old days. Just seeing their faces revived the faulty Heart Logic and Private Conclusions that came with her intense shame. The old, familiar little t truths started running through her head again: "You are such a screw-up." "Try to impress them, so they forget who you used to be." "Run away!" and "The best solution is to get drunk." She knew better than to listen, but she was tempted—and that freaked her out! She called me right away and asked, "Am I turning back into the old Bridget again? I sure hope not, but my confidence is shot." She was scared her new story had been erased. I calmly told her, "No. This is just a collision. It's time to embrace it and learn from it." And she did. She reclaimed the Heart Logic that she is enough, reset her mind on the Big T Truth that her value isn't dependent on others' perceptions of her, and reoriented herself with the Big S Strategy to hold her head high because of God's grace. The experience took her deeper into her new story as God wrote her new identity in bold letters on her heart.

God gave her many opportunities disguised as collisions. Thankfully, they didn't all come at once, or she would have been overwhelmed. In His patient love, God gave her one collision at a time, only what she could handle at any moment. She learned from all of them—sometimes quickly but more often slowly, but it didn't matter. In the end she learned the lessons. As God's edits were reinforced more and more in her heart, the collisions came less and less frequently and took less and less time to reset from.

Noticing the Collisions

Before you had a good understanding of the story in your heart, you may not have noticed the collisions, and if we don't notice, it's easy to miss the Holy Spirit's whisper of an alternative. You just keep going along your way, suffering the consequences without seeing the causes.

However, when you wade into the process of discovery, you gain insight, step by step. You notice the collisions, and you take advantage of them. You didn't hear the alarms before, but you hear them now. You're more alert to disproportionate emotional reactions, the enticement of an old coping skill, or the familiar refrain of a little t truth that clues you in that it's time to fight a battle within. When elements of your old story surface, you no longer blindly accept them as the truth. Now, you challenge them and replace them.

You do a much better job at catching collisions if you know what to look for. Know your little t truths. What do they sound like? Know your small s strategies. What do they look like? Let this self-aware-ness act as alarms that tell you it's time to take control. Don't wait until collisions slap you in the face. Hunt them out. Your counselor, mentor, sponsor, or wise friend is indispensable to give you feedback. Are you hearing the same input over and over about something that needs to shift in your life? If so, it's almost certainly a collision that needs your attention.

God uses all kinds of things to get your attention: conflict, dis-appointments, the truth in God's Word, the Holy Spirit's prompting, and the wisdom of a trusted friend. All of these things can cause the collision inside of you that invites you to choose your new story one more time, and as you do, strengthen its hold on your heart.

Let's be honest: Collisions don't feel very good. In fact, they may make you feel really uncomfortable. You'll want to run. After all, that's how you handled inconvenient truth before. But this time it's different. Press on. Lean in. Learn these important lessons. And grow.

We've found that two tools are effective in helping people take big steps forward. The first is a process called Stop, Think, Pray, and the second is your personal message from God.

Stop, Think, Pray

In collisions, you can use a process called *Stop, Think, Pray,* which guides you through practical steps of saying "no" to the old story and "yes" to God's story.

When something is out of alignment in your story (for example, an old Sore Spot is exerting influence) you're probably going to notice by

1) the way you feel (e.g., anxious, condemned, alone, depressed) 2) the thoughts running through your head (little t truths and Life Lessons) or 3) the things you are doing (little s strategies like numbing, hiding, or self-medicating). In any of these scenarios, the way you take control begins with fighting the battle of Big T Truths to conquer little t truths. You need to get yourself centered on the thoughts that quiet your Sore Spot, reassert healthy Heart Logic, and guide Big S strategies.

When you realize you are in the midst of a collision, Stop, Think, Pray gives you the tools to kick out the little t truth and put a Big T Truth in its place. Similarly, when you're tempted to use a small s strategy, Stop, Think, Pray is the process that enables you to replace it with a Big S Strategy.

Let's take a closer look:

Step 1: *Stop*

When a piece of your flawed story shows up, tell yourself, "Stop." You'll catch unwanted Private Conclusions and Life Lessons surfacing. Remember, these are the tightly held assumptions that determine everything you think, feel, say, and do. When you correct your thoughts and center your heart in God's perspective, you're changing the trajectory of your entire story.

At first, you may realize you've been in the midst of a collision for days, and then you stop and arrest your thoughts. Later, you'll notice in an hour or two, then a few minutes, and eventually, you'll notice them as they surface. Be patient; It's a learned skill.

We need to be bold and follow God's commands, such as, "Take every thought captive" (2 Corinthians 10:5) and "Put off your old self" (Ephesians 4:22f).

Generic weapons don't work very well. The personal specificity of this replacement process is what makes it work. Use your growing self-understanding to target the specific little t truths and small s strategies that have led you off course. Attach a warning to each one. Whenever you see them, it's time to Stop!

Here's an example: If a Sore Spot of insecurity has defined your old story, what will you say "no" to?

These little truths might be running through your head:

- "I can't do this."
- "God thinks I'm a failure."

You might be using these small s strategies:

- Playing the comparison game
- Beating yourself up with critical self-talk
- Silencing your voice

When these surface, tell yourself, be bold and definitive: "I'm not going down that road anymore! Those are lies that have kept me from the unhindered life God meant for me."

The more you can articulate the target you're destroying and the goal you're trying to reach, your chance of winning the battle increases. Without specificity, you'll be confused, you'll fight the wrong fight, you'll try to control your feelings instead of dealing with the root issues that cause the feelings, you'll keep resisting the Holy Spirit because you think you know better, you'll self-sabotage, and you'll give up.

Think about the old story of your heart. What's the most nagging little t truth, and what's the most powerful small s strategy? Write a statement that reflects you saying "no" to both of these:

My little t truth: _____

_____

My small s strategy: _____

_____

At first, you'll probably feel very awkward when you say "no" to any part of the old story. It's all you've ever known, and you've been confident (until now) that it's the right story for you. Fight through the awkwardness. Get support from those who have been down this road before you, and keep moving forward toward God's story of strength and beauty for you.

To be honest, this is where most people stop the process of taking thoughts captive and wonder why it didn't work. Saying "no" to the old is a big step, and they assume it's the only step they need to take. But "nature abhors a vacuum," and if they don't replace those false-hoods and misguided strategies, they'll certainly go back to their old habits. That's why step two is critical.

Step 2: *Think*

In this step, you focus on the "yes"—Big T Truths, Big S Strategies, and God Lessons. These are the good and healthy alternatives, and they have the credibility of God's purposes, the Spirit's power, and the testimony of people who have seen God do amazing things in their lives.

As you Think, you're continuing to follow the command of 2 Corinthians 10:5 to make your thoughts "obedient to Christ" and the command of Ephesians 4:24 to "put on the new self."

In this step, you ask yourself, "What does God want me to say 'yes' to?"

Earlier, we identified the stark differences between little t truth and Big T Truth, and we looked at the contrasts between small s strategies and Big S strategies. This exercise clarifies the choices. If you need more help to remember what God wants you to say "yes" to, ask yourself these questions:

1. "What's the wise thing to do?"

"Before every person lies a road that seems to be right, but at the end of that road death and destruction wait" (Proverbs 16:25, Voice).

The wrong questions are, "What feels right?" and "What do I want?" What we want and how we feel may be the guiding principles our culture uses, but that's not the way it works in our walks with God.

The wise way is God's way. There's a truth (Big T), and there's a way (Big S), and they're often in opposition to what we want or feel. That's what "dying to self" and "being raised in Christ" looks like.

2. "Am I making myself an exception?"

When you need to decide which direction to go, watch for the ways you try to make yourself the exception to some aspect of God's ways and truth. It's normal to look for a parachute, and this is one of the most common—but don't bail out!

You can use these questions in the moments of collision to clarify your choices.

To mean anything, the messages you say "yes" to must be personal. They have to speak directly into your story, and they must carry authority, so remind yourself of God's power.

If you struggle with grace and you depend on your performance for acceptance with God and with people, God is asking you to Think: "I have worth and significance because I'm loved fiercely, and it's got nothing to do with my performance. It's got everything to do with Jesus."

If you're in the grip of fear, God is asking you to Think: "My faith is bigger than my fear because God is on my side."

And if you're battling with insecurity, God is asking you to Think: "I'm valuable because God considers me to be His treasure, and the Holy Spirit lives inside me. I can go forward with holy boldness!"

Think about the old and new stories of your heart. Write a statement of truth that captures what you will say "yes" to:

_____

_____

_____

This, too, is a learned skill—not one that comes easily. Don't be surprised if your learning curve is steep, but stay on it! That's why it needs to have the spiritual authority of God's truth—so you can't argue with it! You need to attach one or two meaningful scriptures to your godly alternative to give it power in your moment of weakness.

Identify two scriptures that give authority and strength to your "yes":

1. _____

_____

2. _____

_____

When you Stop, you have the opportunity to put a stop to the old direction. When you Think, you choose to see things from God's perspective, identify the "yes," and realign your heart with it. But you need more. You need the supernatural power of God unleashed through prayer.

Step 3: *Pray*

The power of prayer propels you in the new direction.

In prayer you claim God's alternative as yours. Take ownership! Come boldly to the throne of grace. Instead of praying, "God, help me believe you love me," pray, "God, I claim right now that you love me! Thank you. Thank you!"

In prayer, you lean into God's strength to help you get beyond the allure of the old way. Call on God's strength. The Holy Spirit lives in you and is ready to make you capable.

You can pray a prayer something like this:

"God, I just said 'no' to this old thought and this old way. You're trying to teach me something new. I claim this new way because it's of you. Provide me with a strength that's beyond my own. I know you will. Thank you!"

For me (Charity) it sounds like this:

"God, I just said 'no' to doubting myself and silencing myself. You've made me bold, and I'll choose to be bold even when I don't feel it. Fill me with your Spirit and give me with your words to speak as I open my mouth. Thank you for making me more than I am on my own!"

Trust God's Word, Not Your Feelings

As you learn the process of Stop, Think, Pray, don't let your feelings rule! There are certain times when you can trust your feelings, but this isn't one of them.

When you feel afraid, fear's voice sounds legitimate. When you feel unsure, insecurity's voice sounds wise. When you feel embarrassed, shame's voice seems to have ultimate authority. Don't listen!

Feelings don't determine truth. God's Word does that. And your feelings don't have to overpower you. You can choose to trust God's Word and ways more than your feelings.

However, realize that it's okay if you can't shake off all of the old feelings, even when you choose a new direction in the midst of a collision. Sometimes, we have to choose the new direction *in spite of* our feelings, especially in the early days when it's all new and unfamiliar. You may still have some anxiety as you say, "I will trust you, God." You may still have some trepidation after you pass up an opportunity that could have brought more success, and say, "I will stop judging myself by my performance." The victory is found in not leaning into the fear and allowing it to paralyze you or propel you in the old direction. The victory is found in embracing the collision, choosing to Stop, Think, Pray, and saying "Yes, Lord, I will follow you into the new direction no matter how I feel." As time goes on, your feelings like fear, trepidation, doubt, and anger will begin to subside, and your heart will learn that it's safe in the new direction you've chosen.

The Power of Stop, Think, Pray

When we introduce Stop, Think, Pray to people, we often hear, "Oh, I already do that." What they mean is that they try distracting themselves from the things they don't want to think and try to think something positive instead.

Stop, Think, Pray is so much more than that! It's a targeted replacement process (designed specifically for you) that rewrites the elements of the old story with God's beautiful love, power, and purpose. It brings you back to the original manuscript in the critical moments when you have to choose between the old story and the new, rewritten one.

To practice Stop, Think, Pray, you need a modicum of self-awareness and a little knowledge of God's Word. It can be done in as little as 20 seconds (once you get really good at it), and it can be done anywhere at any time around anyone. You can use it countless times throughout the day.

It's not a one-size-fits-all approach. Instead, it speaks directly into your heart's story, and it has biblical authority. It's not just a process of wishing and hoping. It gives you a strategy, and a strategy is everything in battle.

Stop, Think, Pray interrupts the perpetual loop of the old story. When God's alternative is put in place of faulty Private Conclusion, it comes with energy that propels you in a new direction. Distraction and positive thinking can't achieve that.

There are a thousand moments in your day when you can use Stop, Think, Pray. When you start to pay attention, you'll increasingly notice how many thoughts, assumptions, and behaviors are rooted in the old story. But you don't have to tackle them all at once. Just start with one, then a couple, and then a few more. Master them and then go for more until God's alternatives become wonderfully normal.

In this process, God may bring up some deep wounds that need to be healed. Perhaps you need to face a trauma, forgive someone of a terrible offense, and interpret past events through God's perspective. Then, practicing Stop, Think, Pray will come more easily because you won't be trying to overcome such a hurdle.

In moments of collision, Stop, Think, Pray is your most effective weapon against lies and the best balm for healing. After a few weeks of practice, you'll likely look back and see a long obedience developing in your new direction.

A Personalized Prayer or Message

Two weapons in the battle are a written prayer or a personalized message that centers you in your new direction. The prayer is your heartfelt praise and request for God to do what only He can do, and the message is what you sense He wanted to say to you—just like the one I (John) shared at the end of Chapter 8.

- A prayer: Take time to think, to reflect on passages of Scripture that are most meaningful to you, and then to write your prayer. Begin with reflections on God being your loving Abba, thank Him for His grace poured out on you in Jesus' sacrifice, thank Him, too, for all the gifts He has given you, and then ask Him to work powerfully to transform your story. For inspiration, you might look at some of the Psalms or Paul's prayers in Ephesians 1, Ephesians 3, and Colossians 1.

- The message: We need to do more than react to the threats to our security in Christ. We also have to be proactive. You can write a personalized message built on God's perspective that reminds you of who you are what is required of you.

This message reminded me (and still reminds me) of God's new direction for me. For months, I read the letter every morning. If I found any internal resistance, I took time to surrender my heart, my desires, my expectations, and my path to God and reset my heart on my new Big T Truth and Big S strategies.

The words in your personal message aren't just random words strung together. They're highly personal words gleaned from intimate moments spent with your Father.

Perhaps you've already begun crafting a letter like this or you've chosen to write out a prayer of declaration as you worked through the personal reflection at the end of Chapter 8. If not, I hope you'll take that opportunity now as you see even more value in creating a tool that centers you in God's message to you.

Protecting the New Story

As people become equipped for the battle, some are still anxious about sustaining what they've begun. They doubt they can really change, and they haven't seen enough progress to encourage them. In fact, as they've become aware of the web of pain and lies in their hearts, they feel they've gone backward! But they haven't. Their fear is a sign they're more objective than ever. Others are convinced the change they see is real, but they're afraid it won't last. They believe the gains will be lost when the chaos of life overwhelms them again.

Yes, it's easy to quit, and yes, it's tempting to find excuses to stop trying. Watch out for the moments of hopelessness and helplessness that try to convince you it's not ever going to get easier. You have to remember that God often calls us into process healing instead of miraculous healing, and our perseverance in the process is essential to accomplishing God's purpose for us. You have to keep putting in the work! When Jesus met a paralyzed man at the pool of Bethesda, the man had been waiting for years to be healed. Jesus asked him, "Do you want to get well?" (John 5:6) He's asking you the same question.

You have to make your heart's health a priority in a schedule that's already full of priorities. You'll have to create margin so you can pay attention and reset your direction back toward God's new story. Silence, solitude, and self-reflection need to be your frequent companions. You have to fiercely protect what God has done and is doing in you. When it starts feeling better for a few weeks, don't back off. Relaxing too much too soon in the process of healing fails to respect the fragility of new gains.

Remember that Stop, Think, Pray and your personalized message are your insurance policy against slipping. They are the most important tools to keep your heart centered in God's story because they call you back to the truths that heal the old pain. They quiet the influence of events and people that can trigger the pain of Sore Spots. And they remind you of God's personal, intimate, and life-giving message. Lean into these two tools and let them quiet your fears.

However, you're going to need other good disciplines to support you in this battle. As you use these tools, add good habits of regular Bible reading, prayer that taps into God's love and power, and community. Another way to say it is this: To make progress, we need the Word of God, the Spirit of God, and at least a few wise people of God. Give these people permission to ask hard questions and speak into your life. For example, have them regularly ask you the four Heart Logic questions, and invite them to ask if you're on track with Big S Strategies. Let them help you measure your Life Outcomes as a sign of how well you're walking in your new direction.

You also need to stay in good soul care rhythms that allow space and time to pay attention to your heart. Regularly look inward and take inventory. Take a few moments at the end of the day to identify where collisions occurred and how you fared. Be aware of new pain and reconcile it to the new story God is writing on your heart.

All of these disciplines give you strength, energy, and wisdom for the battle. Don't neglect them, especially when you feel especially vulnerable or discouraged.

In Chapter 10, we saw the parallel between heart surgery and the process of having God rewrite your heart's story, and we pointed out the importance of aftercare when people leave the hospital. Let's look more closely at an aftercare plan for you:

The "Aftercare" Plan:

1) Read your personalized message that represents what God wants you to remember every morning to start your day. Take time to absorb the meaning of each part.

2) In the moments of collision, fight the battle of the mind with Stop, Think, Pray.

3) Stay engaged in prayer and Scripture reading. Use some of the time you spend in these disciplines to reinforce the new story for your heart.

4) Find an accountability partner who will ask about the elements of your story.

5) Begin a self-reflection journal to monitor your thoughts and actions. How many little t thoughts were present today? How many small s strategies were present today? How well did you replace them?

6) Engage in soul care. Manage your daily rhythm so you have margin and capacity to invest in your heart. Make silence, solitude, and self-reflection your regular companions.

Reflection

What are some collisions you've noticed as you've read the book?

How did you respond to them?

What will prompt you to Stop? Craft a statement that sums it up.

What are some specific thoughts that will need to be replaced? What truths will replace them?

Describe the difference between a weakly expressed prayer and one that boldly claims God's promises.

Have you tried to fight the battle with unwanted thoughts before? How might using Stop, Think, Pray help you fight more effectively?

Review the aftercare plan. Write your specific strategy to fulfill each element.

What are some ways an aftercare plan is essential for continued growth?

It's important to internalize and normalize the concept of a partnership with God. Instead of waiting for Him to do it all, or leaving Him out and trying to make life work yourself, you've been finding the blend between His part and yours. How will this be important going forward in an aftercare plan?

The Story of Your Heart Writes the Story of Your Life.

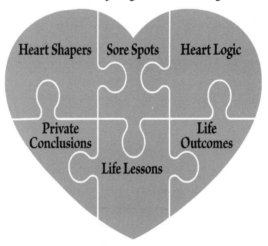

CHAPTER 12

Living in Your New Story

You have established a new relationship with the powers of darkness. Whatever you were before you were a Christian, you are now a sworn foe of the legions of hell. Have no delusions about their reality or their hostility, but do not fear them. The God inside you terrifies them. They cannot touch you, let alone hurt you, but they can still seduce, and they will try. They will also oppose you as you obey Christ. [Because] you are serious about Christ being your Lord and God, you can expect opposition.

—JIM CYMBALA

In the battle, your heart will be your enemy . . . at least, in the beginning. It will fight for what feels safe and known—your old story. For many years, your mind has been listening to the voice of little t truth and Life Lessons and the shouts of your pain. Your heart is wounded, and it lashes out at any perceived threat—like the truth of God's love. As you take steps forward, be kind to yourself because you have so much to overcome, but at the same time, be ruthless to root out the lies and replace them with truth.

As you win daily skirmishes, you'll gradually trust more in God's grace, truth, and power, and you'll be able to relax a bit more instead of frantically trying to prove yourself, hiding from threats, or intimidating people to control them. Your perception of people, God, and events becomes more accurate, and hope will increasingly replace fear.

Your heart will start working with you rather than against you. At some point, it'll protect the new story as fiercely as it's protected the old. The internal resistance will fade, you'll recognize the devil's voice, and you won't have to work so hard anymore. (But remember, don't stop your disciplines too soon.) You'll enjoy more wisdom, joy, and strength than you ever thought possible.

As time goes by, the new normal will eventually begin to feel normal. Yes, it will happen!

A man who has always covered his insecurity with bravado convinced himself that his domineering manner is a sign of his exemplary leadership. He married a woman who wanted someone to run her life for her, but she resented being told what to do all the time. One of his three children was terrified of him and complied with his every wish, even before he spoke it. Another started using drugs to numb the pain of feeling unloved, and the third was defiant (much like his father). When he began to partner with God to rewrite his story, he felt like he was living outside of his own skin. He tried to see things more objectively, but the patterns of dominating people to feel safe were deeply embedded in him. After a few months, his heart began to soften; he actually wept when he felt the pain he had suppressed so long. His honest emotions and his new path shook up the family and the people who reported to him at the office. They had a hard time believing the change was real, but it was. He began to feel more comfortable, to listen, to care, and to respond to problems without blowing up. After a year, there are only a few glimpses of his former story. People love the new man, and instead of reacting to him in fear or defiance, they move toward him in love. His bravado is still there to some extent, but it's tempered with kindness and patience. He was a good leader with big flaws before, and now he's a great leader whose transformed flaws have become the source of his genius. He's found a new normal in his new story.

As you step into your new normal, it will take thought, effort, and intentionality in the beginning. I know that sounds exhausting. You're already tired from the toll your broken ways have taken on you! But hold on to this promise: All of the effort it took to get you to the wrong place will be erased by a double dose of God's blessings. The Spirit will breathe relief, freedom, and health into you day by day.

John Ortberg said of Dallas Willard, "What drew me to Dallas was the sense that here was someone who had mastered the inner life—or had at least gone farther down the road than most. There was a leisure of spirit to him."[21] "Leisure of spirit" sounds like someone who experienced the truth of God deep in his heart and reveled in the overwhelming peace it generates. Dr. Willard must have done the work to have God's version of the story written in his heart.

Let God rewrite your story, too, and give leisure to your heart.

---

21 John Ortberg, *Soul Keeping*, p. 39.

Your Emerging Genius

As your story is being rewritten, an incredible work of art is emerging—it's your full potential, your emerging genius. In Chapter 4, we saw that your true genius isn't your intelligence, your ability to succeed, or your capacity to innovate. We believe God's definition of genius is living to the full capacity of your spiritual DNA. It is revealed when God's original story is returned to your heart and you cross your gap into your unhindered life.

In Chapter 4 we saw how the site of wounding became the source of genius for the disciple Peter after he denied Christ. He had been impulsive; he became measured. He had been proud; he became humble. He had been foolish; he became wise. He had been too sure of himself; he became teachable for the rest of his life.

As you walk down a new road, your genius will show up more. You might say, "I didn't know I had this in me!" I (Charity) have made this statement many times over the years. As I explained earlier, I was the shy kid who once lived by the Life Lessons: "Don't show your heart," and "Hold back and let other people lead." But I've learned to live by the God Lesson: "Show your holy boldness!" I sometimes scratch my head and ask, "Who is this girl?" That's the genius in me coming alive. My emerging genius doesn't make me better than anyone else. It simply makes me the best version of myself so I can be used by God for His glory. It also doesn't put unachievable expectations on me. I have "realistic zeal"—a passion to make a difference coupled with the realization that I'm a "broken pot" (2 Corinthians 4:7).

Your new story brings you a step closer to the image of Jesus. You love more deeply. You trust more readily. You lean on your wisdom more than your untrustworthy feelings. You don't run from conflict, but instead, you engage with a beautiful blend of grace and truth. You let go of your agenda and join God on His amazing, yet unpredictable journey. You draw more deeply from the well of the Spirit's love and power, and you have more of an impact for Jesus.

Every time you take a step closer to Jesus, you breathe a sigh of relief because His ways are free and light (Matthew 11:28-30, MSG). Life is so much easier when you aren't working against yourself!

Your Unhindered Life

As your genius emerges, it leads you to an unhindered life. Life becomes sweeter when your story is rewritten. You'll craft your life so that the outcomes really are better. You'll be attracted to healthier people and healthier circumstances. Life will probably be a lot more pleasant, hopeful, and blessed than ever before.

Of course, God doesn't guarantee that life will always be smooth and easy. After all, Jesus' life was anything but smooth and easy! We're called to follow Him, so we can expect some opposition and setbacks, but we can also expect God to give us a sense of purpose in every twist and turn in the story. It may not be easy, but we'll experience an amazing sense of freedom that we've never known before. We know that more pain is on its way. But when we encounter pain with God's rewritten story in our hearts, we'll have more resilience. We'll celebrate God's blessings and face difficulties with patience and faith.

Blessed So You Can Bless

All of this work to rewrite your story isn't just a selfish pursuit. God uses your pain to deepen your faith and expand your compassion—He is blessing you to be a blessing.

As we've seen, we won't make progress as long as we try to hide the pain and make excuses for those who hurt us. In their book, *The Cure*, John Lynch, Bruce McNichol, and Bill Thrall remind us to have the courage to be honest: "Unhealed wounds require our attention and we will have trouble focusing on others while those wounds still need attention. This causes many of us to miss our destinations, on a routine basis, that over a lifetime produce our destiny."[22]

In Matthew 10:9-10 (MSG), Jesus refers to the disciples as the "equipment," referring to them as His instruments of change. The same can be said of you: You are God's equipment. God is rewriting your story and expanding your capacity to make a difference in the lives of others. The lid comes off and you can go to the next level of impact. You're free to run with perseverance the race marked out for you (Hebrews 12:1). The love and strength that's growing in you will flow through you to bless others.

You'll listen and respond when God prompts you to share Jesus with your neighbor. You won't be held back by insecurity. You'll be ready to trust Him when He asks you to move across the country for a job. You won't be held back by fear. You'll be willing to forgive your family member who has hurt you so deeply, demonstrating God's grace instead of putting up walls. The impact you make on the lives of others will mirror the impact God has made in your life.

22 John Lynch, Bruce McNichol, and Bill Thrall, *The Cure: What If God Isn't Who You Think He Is and Neither are You?* (Phoenix: Trueface, 2011).

God often uses what He's taught us to speak directly into the lives of others who are still living their old stories. As we experience God's comfort, we can comfort others. As you recall, that was Paul's experience: "Praise be to the God and Father of our Lord Jesus Christ, the Father of compassion and the God of all comfort, who comforts us in all our troubles, so that we can comfort those in any trouble with the comfort we ourselves receive from God" (2 Corinthians 1:3-4).

That's certainly true for me. God has used what He's taught me about finding my boldness to speak empowerment into the lives of others who, like me, have been held back by self-doubt or timidity. He has also used what He's taught me about overcoming the desires of the flesh and leaning into the power of the Spirit to help others choose a path of sobriety.

I have no doubt that God has someone in your path who will be blessed by the gifts He has given you!

Count on it: What God is doing in you will flow through you!

Dare to dream. Don't hold back. Follow Jesus to incredible adventures. Run without hindrances the race God has marked out for you. You're being blessed so that you might bless others.

Reflection

Now, at the end of the book, what are you feeling about the opportunity for God to edit your life's story? Excited, hopeful, apprehensive, confused, or some other emotion?

Do you have confidence that God has the love, wisdom, and power to turn your pain into the platform for your greatest impact on people? Explain your answer.

Take a moment to dream of unhindered life that's being created in you and through you. What does it look like?

How will you become a greater blessing to people around you and perhaps to people around the world?

What's your next step? What's God's next step?

Appendices

Appendix A. How Trust and Hope Come from Rewriting Heart Logic

1) Is God good? Is He really good all the time?

	TRUST	HOPE
YES	You trust God. You're able to follow His will. You're willing to take risks. You believe you will be okay, even in very difficult circumstances.	You find hope through trust in God's sovereignty. You have hope in God's eternal promises that are bigger than our broken lives. You pray fiercely for help when you need it, believing God is with you.

NO	You don't trust God. You may be self-reliant and more defiant toward God than you realize. You struggle to see purpose in pain.	You have no hope that God has a bigger plan. In fact, you wait for Him to burn you. You can't see the purpose in your pain, especially when it may not be revealed until later down the road.

2) Am I good even though I'm flawed? Am I valued and am I truly worthy of love?

	TRUST	HOPE
YES	You trust in who God made you to be. You walk with your head held high because the God of the universe considers you to be His treasure. You're self-assured. You can strive for excellence without pursuing perfectionism.	You can hope in your ability to learn and grow. You can give yourself grace along the way. You see hope in making it beyond your gap.

NO	You don't trust in who God made you to be. You're insecure and second-guess yourself. You strive for unattainable perfection, never feeling like standards are met. You work too hard for worth and value. You may be self-critical and overly sensitive to criticism. You may be timid.	Shame dominates your thoughts and emotions. You have no hope of being more than you are right now. You're very hard on yourself. You feel helpless and worthless. You fall into the gap.

3) Are other people good? Is there really goodness among the brokenness in humanity?

	TRUST	HOPE
YES	You value vulnerability, openness, collaboration, and teamwork. You have the ability to forgive.	You believe other people have positive motivations, even when they mess up. You hope in others' abilities to learn and grow from their mistakes.

NO	You put up walls, avoid being vulnerable, and control things yourself. You hold grudges and resentments. You worry a lot about others' intentions and motivations. You expect the worst from others.	You have no hope in people. In fact, you may not have much use for them. You have a hard time seeing beyond people's mistakes or the times they burned you.

4) Is life good? Is life good even in the most difficult times?

	TRUST	HOPE
YES	You trust God will bring you through. You trust He has a purpose in your pain, even if you don't see it yet.	You have hope in what's to come. You have resilience, the ability to rise above hard circumstances. You approach hardship by asking, "God, what are you teaching me?"
NO	You don't trust there's any purpose in your pain. You get overwhelmed by the struggles. Life feels really hard—too hard.	You feel hopeless in the chaos. You give up, feel helpless, and become overwhelmed. You may find yourself depressed when you encounter difficulties because you expect the worst.

Appendix B. Heart Shapers: A Life Timeline

Use the space below to create your own timeline. Mark the decades, and then ask God to remind you of events, both pleasant and painful, that have shaped your life. Write them on the timeline. As you reflect, you may remember events you haven't thought about in a long time. Write them down.

Childhood

_____

_____

_____

_____

_____

_____

_____

_____

Adolescence

_____

_____

_____

_____

_____

_____

_____

_____

_____

Early Adulthood

_____

_____

_____

_____

_____

_____

_____

_____

_____

_____

_____

_____

Middle Adulthood

_____

_____

_____

_____

_____

_____

_____

_____

_____

_____

_____

_____

Late Adulthood

_____

_____

_____

_____

_____

_____

_____

_____

_____

_____

_____

_____

Now, ask yourself two questions:

What positive events and loving people shaped my life?

_____

_____

_____

_____

_____

_____

_____

_____

_____

_____

What painful events and difficult people created Sore Spots?

_____

_____

_____

_____

_____

_____

_____

_____

_____

_____